S0-ABY-196

A Teen
Eating Disorder
Prevention
Book

Understanding Food and Your Family

Clare Tattersall

RJ
506
E18
T38
1999

The Rosen Publishing Group, Inc./New York

Published in 1999 by The Rosen Publishing Group, Inc.
29 East 21st Street, New York, NY 10010

Copyright 1999 by Clare Tattersall

All rights reserved. No part of this book may be reproduced in any form without permission in writing from the publisher, except by a reviewer.

Library of Congress Cataloging-in-Publication Data

Tattersall, Clare.
    Understanding food and your family / Clare Tattersall.
       p.   cm.—(A teen eating disorder prevention book)
    Includes bibliographical references and index.
    Summary: Describes how eating patterns and attitudes about food are partly determined by one's family and discusses eating disorders and how to deal with them.
    ISBN 0-8239-2860-8 (lib. bdg.)
    1. Eating disorders in adolescence—Patients—Family relationships—Juvenile literature. 2. Eating disorders in children—Patients—Family relationships—Juvenile literature. [1. Eating disorders.] I. Title. II. Series.
    RJ506.E18T38 1999
    616.85'26'00835--dc21
    99-13737
    CIP

Manufactured in the United States of America

ABOUT THE AUTHOR

Clare Tattersall is a freelance writer. She writes plays, films, and magazine articles on a wide variety of topics. Her play *The Last Dance* was made into a short film. She lives in New York City.

Contents

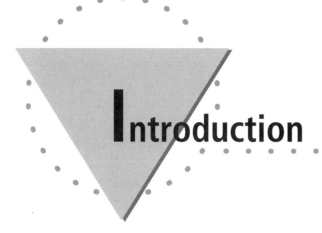

Introduction

"**D**iet, diet, diet." It seems like that's all you ever see and hear. It's there when you switch on the television, read a magazine, look at billboards, eat lunch at school, and have dinner at home.

So just what shape *should* you be? How large? How small? What should food represent? Fuel? Punishment? Reward? Love? How can you learn to eat healthily?

Sometimes it seems as if food is your best friend. Other times it can be your worst enemy. You can punish yourself and the people around you by not eating, or you can binge secretly when no one else is there.

If food means more to you than just fuel, you are not alone. In today's society food has come to represent more than just the nourishment needed to support your body. Many people use food to fill emotional voids in their lives. For many people food takes the place of love.

1

The Social Significance of Food

Millions of years ago, the primary reason for eating was survival. Humans ate in order to stay alive. In many cultures the women gathered fruits and berries, while the men hunted and fished for meat to bring back to the others.

Since then a lot has changed. Food is central to our lives and our perceptions of ourselves: It determines the way we deal with the world. Holidays and celebrations are arranged around it, and families gather together because of it. Food is one of the ways we appreciate other cultures. Creative cooking is often seen as a means of artistic expression. Food can indicate wealth or poverty. The way we behave in our relationships is frequently affected by it. Food can be used either as punishment or reward, and sometimes it is a test of self-control. It can bring us attention, or we can hide behind it. Food plays many roles in our lives.

FOOD AND SOCIETY

Hunger is a response to your body's needs. Food provides all of the necessary vitamins, minerals, proteins, carbohydrates, and fats that we need to stay alive. When you eat, your hunger is satisfied. But society has placed such enormous importance on food that when you eat, you are dealing with many complex issues that have nothing to do with your basic nutritional needs.

Home

At home you probably eat most meals with your family. A family meal can be a social event. You exchange news about what happened during the day. You talk about your hopes, and you trade views and opinions. You probably have a special seat to sit in, and you always see your family from this same position.

Maybe you argue or feel uncomfortable at mealtimes. It is possible that you feel pressured or sense a negative atmosphere. Good or bad mealtimes are significant events in your daily life.

Social Gatherings

At parties, weddings, funerals, or other social gatherings, food is almost always part of the agenda. It is laid out in a decorative style. It is there not for nutritional value but rather to look attractive. Food can be used for many purposes at social gatherings, including decoration, tradition, and celebration.

Going Out to Eat

Your parents or relatives may like to go out to dinner. They may spend lots of money in expensive restaurants where they can show off their manners and good taste. Or perhaps they prefer fast-food restaurants, which are springing up everywhere. These are good for an inexpensive bite to eat or when you don't have time for a proper meal. Sometimes they are a treat or a special place to go. They help us to live a "life on the run."

Different Cultures

In different cultures people celebrate different holidays, but food is often central to those celebrations, either in the form of feast or fast.

For instance, Thanksgiving is centered around one large meal shared with family and friends. Many cultural groups in the United States and Canada, such as Greeks, Jews, and Italians, celebrate with feasts that last a whole day. Christians enjoy a big, traditional meal on Christmas Day.

During other holidays, such as Yom Kippur and Ramadan, people show devotion and respect by fasting, or not eating, from sunup to sundown.

LEARNING TO EAT

We are first introduced to food as babies. When you were a baby, the only way you could ask for anything was to cry. You cried if you were hungry or tired or uncomfortable, and your mother or caretaker had to figure out what you needed.

Parents do their best, but they are not superhuman;

sometimes they get it wrong. Your caretaker may have thought that you were crying because you were hungry and fed you. He or she may have gotten up several times in the middle of the night to feed you, in addition to all the times during the day when you cried.

Chances are that you were fed when you were not hungry. As a result, you started to learn that the giving and receiving of food was an important family connection. You learned to trust your parents, and this trust was rooted in food.

FOOD CAN SYMBOLIZE MANY THINGS

Independence

In some tribal societies, teenage boys and girls go through certain rituals to become men or women and claim their independence. In the United States or Canada, you might graduate from high school and start work, or you might go to college. You might live at home, or you might not. It is difficult for your parents, who have spent years caring for you and giving you the equipment they think you need to deal with the world, to see you use that equipment to establish your independence. This struggle often causes resentment and anger.

When Maxine went to university, her parents were happy because she was the first person in the family ever to go to college. When she came home for the holidays, they were pleased to see her but surprised by the bag of brown rice in her suitcase and the vegetarian cookbook under her arm. That night she did not want to eat the same red meat and potatoes that everyone else was having.

"If it's good enough for us, it's good enough for you," her father muttered under his breath.

Maxine went straight to her room and did not join in family meals for the rest of her visit. She would wait until they had finished eating and then make herself a light meal of salad, rice, and lentils.

"What's wrong with you?" her mother pleaded.

Nothing is wrong with Maxine. She is just establishing her independence, breaking away from the family traditions by opting for a different type of food. Maxine is becoming an independent young woman, and food is part of that process.

A Woman's Role

Women and girls often feel pressured to nurture, care for, and love others. TV commercials and magazines are full of exciting tips and recipes on how to make nutritious, healthy, attractive food for other people. Commercials in particular indicate that a woman's value is based upon her ability to provide love, which usually means providing food.

The message is that the enticing food you see is not for you. It is to give but not to eat yourself, because food will make you fat. Your value is determined by others who give approval or disapproval depending upon your size. Early in life you learn that to be thin is to be accepted. So eating food represents health and happiness for other people, but for you it signifies failure.

The offering of food has lost its original meaning of providing health and nutrition and has come to symbolize love, care, approval, the expression of feelings, comfort, and apology.

What About Boys?

In today's world, the media's focus on thinness and beauty generally applies mostly to women. Appearance—and weight in particular—is usually seen as a feminine issue. But boys too, especially athletes, have fears about their weight.

Raoul, a ninth grader, was on the junior varsity basketball team, but he felt constant pressure to do better. His father was pleased that Raoul was on the team but didn't accept that as enough. He wanted his son to be the team captain. He took Raoul to extra training sessions and put him on a strict diet.

The coach kept warning Raoul about his weight. He said that unless Raoul shed some extra pounds, he wouldn't be allowed on the team next year.

Raoul was afraid of letting both his family and coach down. He put himself on an even stricter diet and introduced his own new, rigorous training schedule. The pounds dropped away, and at first Dad and the coach were pleased with Raoul. But his buddies on the team made fun of him. They called him "skinny girl" and "Raoulita."

Raoul had started to diet in order to please the adults around him, but as he lost weight, he was seen differently by his friends. He then increased his combination of diet and exercise to cope with the confusion he was feeling. A year later, Raoul's father became very worried about his son's obsessive behavior, and together they agreed that Raoul should see a therapist, someone he could talk to freely about his confused feelings.

Both boys and girls can suffer from eating disorders.

Boredom

Brenda's father is taking her out for the day. Usually when they spend the day together, they go to the movies or a museum. But today they are going to the car dealership. Brenda does not know why she has to go along and is angry with her father. He seems to be taking ages to look at the cars, and he can never make up his mind. Brenda is left in the office with the secretary. She kicks her foot again and again against the corner of the desk. Why doesn't Dad come and save her from her boredom? she wonders.

"Here, have a candy," says the secretary, offering her a box of chocolates. Brenda takes one. A few minutes later she takes another. Brenda eats almost all of the chocolates before her father makes his decision and they can leave the office.

As Brenda gets older, she finds that she can lose herself in food. When she is bored and has nobody to talk to or nothing to do, she knows that food will distract her.

Using food as relief from boredom is not a solution. Food can't help you to escape from your feelings, it can only distract you for a short time. Instead of looking for something to eat, try to find an activity to take your mind away from food. Go for a walk, call a friend, or read a book. There are lots of fun and productive things to do besides eat.

Expressing Emotion

It seemed to Dave as if his father was always telling him what to do: "Go and clean the car." "Get out of the house for a while." "Go help your sisters." "Do the dishes." Yet he never seemed to get anything in return for all of this. His father hardly ever let him use the car, and he never listened to him.

Finally Dave's father promised that he could have the car. Dave was going to drive his buddies around instead of being driven like usual. He made all of the arrangements: when, where, who. But at the last minute, his father changed his mind.

Dave was furious. Didn't his father understand what a fool he was making of him? Now he would have to call everyone back and cancel. His father wouldn't listen to reason. Dave did not know what he could do to be heard.

He went into the kitchen and grabbed some leftover pizza from the refrigerator. He stuffed it into his mouth and barely chewed it. He ate until his anger died down, then went to his room and lay on his bed.

Dave was frustrated and did not know how to express his feelings. He had often seen his mother, in a fury, take a bag of cookies or potato chips into her bedroom and come out later in a much better mood.

Dave ate to repress his feelings because he did not have an outlet to release them. But dealing with anger in this way is not a solution. Dave still felt resentment toward his father. It is sometimes difficult to deal with situations where parents or people in authority do not allow you to voice your feelings. Calmly telling them what is on your mind, or even writing them a letter to explain how their actions make you feel, is a first step toward improving communication.

FOOD IS NOT A SOLUTION

Food is only one way of showing love. It cannot fix your problems. Starving yourself or bingeing are not effective ways of comforting yourself when you feel unloved, lonely, confused, angry, or miserable. It may seem to help at first, but it only makes your situation worse by adding guilt or regret to your list of painful feelings.

Food can never fill an emotional void. Overcoming negative feelings requires strength and bravery. It requires that you talk to your parents or friends, express your feelings when they have been hurt, and work to fill the emptiness with new, healthy emotions.

Words are for feelings; food is for nourishment.

EATING RITUALS

Eating rituals in families have no limits to their variations. They are as diverse and individual as the people themselves. There are, however, a few common rituals that can, and often do, have devastating results.

Glen's mom has an after-dinner ritual. Every evening after they have cleared away the dishes and are sitting in front of the television, she asks, "Can I get anyone something else to eat?" If nobody responds, she applies the power of suggestion. "Ice cream, maybe?" she asks, but everyone has just finished eating a filling meal, with dessert included. "An apple or an orange?" she offers.

Mom has no takers. Disappointed, she pulls out a candy bar and bites into it. "It's really good," she says. "Are you sure you wouldn't like one?"

Glen looks over at his mom and feels sorry for her. She is somewhat overweight and knows she should not be eating chocolate. Glen is not hungry, but...

"Okay," he says. His mom, excited that someone is going to eat with her and share her guilt, runs off to the kitchen and brings back two candy bars.

Glen's mom is showing him that food is a substitute for love, and by taking the candy bars, Glen accepts her love.

Abdul likes to eat at his grandmother's house when his mother is angry or too busy for him. His grandmother spends the entire day preparing a huge, elaborate meal, just in case one of her children or grandchildren stops by.

Abdul's parents are divorced, and his father lives in Florida. Once a month he flies north to visit Abdul. They go to baseball games together and eat hot dogs. They see movies and eat popcorn, and they always stop at McDonald's for a cheeseburger afterward.

When Abdul feels neglected by his mother, his grandmother fills him with snacks. And Abdul's dad is showing him that he loves and misses him by treating him to an excess of unhealthy junk food.

Sandy's story is different. She is sixteen, and her parents are splitting up. Every evening the three of them sit down for a family meal, and inevitably her parents fight. They fight about Sandy, and they fight about themselves. There is never a happy, peaceful meal in their house. Even the sight of food makes Sandy feel upset and angry.

Sandy has learned to associate mealtimes with anger and pain. As a result, she tries to avoid eating altogether.

WHAT EATING RITUALS DOES YOUR FAMILY HAVE?

⊙ Think about your family's eating rituals. How do they affect the way you think about food?

⊙ Write a short paragraph about your family meals. Do you enjoy them? What is the general atmosphere? How does this make you feel? Do you tend to eat a large or small amount?

⊙ Do you eat between meals? Is this encouraged in your family? Why or why not?

⊙ What eating rituals do your friends have? Do they have habits that you find strange? Why do you think they have these habits?

⊙ What does food mean to you? Do you ever eat in secret? How did you learn this behavior? How do you feel before, during and after you do this?

⊙ Do you like to eat in public? Do you sometimes feel pressured to eat? How do you deal with this?

⊙ How does your family treat food? Do you eat candy or junk food when you are not hungry? Think about the times you eat and why.

2 How Eating Patterns Develop

You develop your first eating patterns as a baby; you cry when you are hungry, and your caretaker feeds you. As you grow older, you start to make associations between food and your feelings. Perhaps mealtimes are happy events in your family, when you come together to talk.

Or maybe they represent fear, hurt, or anger. One young woman remembers her parents' endless fights at mealtimes in the year before their divorce. She felt alone and scared in the midst of their arguments.

Maybe you associate your neighbors or grandparents with edible treats—food used as a symbol of comfort and affection. Maybe you associate food with punishment or reward: a way to learn right and wrong, pride or guilt.

Just as you learn your eating patterns from your family, their own habits originated in their childhood and the patterns that they learned. If they have happy memories of food and eating, they will try to pass these on to you, but if they have bad memories, they may try to correct them. Unfortunately, parents sometimes err too far in the opposite direction and end up doing harm.

WHEN FOOD IS SCARCE

Rudy's parents are German but moved to America before Rudy was born. They grew up during the war, when food was scarce. They had rationing booklets that they took to the store, which allowed them only a small amount of eggs, fruit, and vegetables every week. Meat was rare, and candy was almost unheard of. When Rudy's parents moved to America, they worked hard to build a new life for themselves and make sure that their kids never went without.

Rudy's parents were very successful in America. His mom quit her job and stayed home every day to look after her son. She had spare time on her hands now and a lot of money to spend. She loved to buy expensive chocolates and other delicacies. As Rudy grew up, his mom always made sure that he had plenty of food on his plate and that his pockets were full of candy. Often she would bake him a special cheesecake or pecan pie when he came in from school. Rudy would often eat when he was not hungry because he could see how much it meant to his mother.

Instead of learning to say, "No thank you, but I still love you," Rudy learned that food meant love.

He felt that by refusing the snacks his mother offered, he would be refusing her love. He learned that he couldn't say no to food without feeling as though he was hurting someone's feelings and rejecting them.

FOOD AS PUNISHMENT

Nadia sat down to eat and found an over-cooked bean burger and two boiled potatoes on her plate. "Uh oh, Mom's mad," she thought, but she did not know what was wrong.

"Have I been bad?" she asked, but was met with stony silence. Nadia knew that she must have annoyed her mother because a horrible meal of tasteless food was always given out as punishment.

When Nadia was sixteen she noticed that she was punishing herself in the same way. When she did something that she knew was wrong, she only picked at her food that night. When she went away to college, she frequently punished herself for bad grades or failed relationships by starving herself.

Withholding favorite foods, sending a child to bed with no dinner, or forcing him or her to eat cold leftovers for breakfast are punishments used by parents as a tool for shaping behavior. Nadia knew that she had been bad but did not understand why. Mutual understanding is the basis for any healthy family relationship, and you have the right to express your feelings and be told what is expected of you.

Nadia's mother was angry because she had repeatedly asked her daughter to clean her room, and she had forgotten. But Nadia only knew that she must have done something very wrong to have upset her mother so much. Often Nadia knew she had been bad, but didn't understand why. This lack of understanding reinforced her low self-esteem. Eventually Nadia took to punishing herself in the same way.

FOOD AS REWARD

As a child, were you ever given candy after a visit to the doctor? A special trip to the local fast-food joint after a boring shopping trip? A cookie for not making a fuss when you hurt yourself? As kids we are often rewarded with little treats after unpleasant experiences.

As you grow older, it is easy to hold on to this reward system. When dumped by a boyfriend or girlfriend, it is easy to head for the refrigerator in search of comforting foods, which give you the same warm feeling as love.

When Tia left home and moved to a different state to go to college, her life changed. She settled into her dormitory, registered for classes, took a dance lesson—and met Henry.

Tia had had several boyfriends back home; they came and went, and there was always another one. But Henry was different. It was love at first sight. Henry was so romantic. Nobody had ever given her flowers before, but Henry gave her long-stemmed roses. He told her that she was beautiful and one day invited Tia to the college ball.

Yet he never showed up to meet her that night. Tia waited in her room. After half an hour, she started to feel uncomfortable in her new dress. After another half hour, she had tear-stains on her dress. Tia went to the ball alone, and inside she saw Henry. He was dancing with another girl.

"Sorry, but something else came up," he said.

In tears, Tia headed for the buffet. "At least I'll get my money's worth," she thought as she took food from every tempting dish and then returned for seconds on dessert. Didn't she deserve it?

Tia ate and ate. "I need something good in my life," she thought as she devoured her third piece of chocolate cake, "and this is it."

By eating uncontrollably, Tia was both comforting and rewarding herself for dealing with her pain. Her belief in love had been shattered, and she was rewarding herself for surviving.

In her book *Overcoming the Legacy of Overeating*, Nan Fuchs suggests making a "rewards list" every time you find yourself seeking comfort from eating. She recommends that you make a list of ideas or items that you would like instead of food. Think of things that would make you feel happier no matter how far-fetched, such as going to a movie, making a new friend, or vacationing on a tropical island. She then suggests rewarding yourself with whichever alternative is possible.

THE POWER STRUGGLE

Your mom or dad might be strict. Sometimes they may seem overly strict when they want you to behave and think like them.

"Think of all the hungry children in the world," Mary's mother said. "You can't have any dessert until you've finished," her aunt said. But Mary absolutely could not eat her spinach. She hated it. It tasted horrible, and the stalks made her want to gag. She sat at the table after everyone else had left.

Eventually her mother took the plate away and sent her to bed. But when Mary came down for breakfast the next morning, she found a reheated plate of last night's spinach instead of cereal or waffles.

Her mother was playing a power game with her; she was showing Mary who was boss. Mary felt powerless. She ate the spinach, but her stomach heaved with every mouthful.

Mary's feelings of powerlessness against her mother spilled into other areas of her life. She felt as though her choices were often being taken away by someone stronger than her. Later in life when she felt trapped, she would simply give up or give in. Mary's relationship with food had taught her to act submissive in other relationships where she felt powerless.

FOOD AS LOVE

As you have learned, the need for love is commonly expressed through food. Rudy ate the chocolates and cakes that his mother made for him because he recognized that to reject the food would have seemed like a rejection of her love.

Abdul remembers his grandmother's cooking and how secure and comfortable he was at her house when he felt neglected by his mother. He also recalls eating hot dogs and burgers with his father on his visits from Florida.

Our associations with food are formed early in life, and they are mostly associations of love or the lack of it. Feeling unloved is a common theme among people with eating disorders. Rudy binges on sweet fatty foods when he feels alone or insecure. So does Abdul.

Sandra had been sexually abused by her father since she was four years old. She was seventeen when she left home.

Her mother is still unaware of what was happening, and Sandra has always been too afraid to tell her. Sandra feels dirty, ashamed and responsible for the destruction her father said she would cause if she told anyone. She is afraid for her two younger sisters. She does not understand love and feels confused and guilty.

Sandra eats to distance herself from her body. She wants to be ugly so that she will be left alone. Candy provides her with a sense of comfort that she does not have in her life. Eating dulls her senses and gives her a feeling of love—a feeling she does not hate herself for experiencing.

Fortunately, at the age of twenty-two, Sandra is under the care of a rehabilitation center. She is undergoing intensive therapy to help her cope with her eating disorder and her history of abuse. She is creating a new future for herself where she understands love. She is starting to believe that she can establish loving relationships with other people.

Crystal comes from a large family where everyone competes for attention. She is the third child of five and has always been considered the "good" one.

Her older sisters receive attention for their academic and athletic abilities, while her younger sisters get attention because of their rebellious styles and the boyfriends they bring home. Crystal, meanwhile, is quiet and polite. She is also anorexic.

Crystal is struggling to be noticed. She feels unloved and invisible. She wants to be recognized as an individual who is worthy of love, as she feels her sisters are.

During your teens and early twenties, coming to terms and coping with your emotions is hard. You might not feel that you get the support at home that you would like. Maybe food seems to be your only friend when the rest of the world is against you. But it is not. Long-term happiness begins with understanding and liking yourself. It lies in good communication with your family and in learning to express your needs to your parents without being afraid of rejection.

WHAT DOES FOOD SYMBOLIZE IN YOUR FAMILY?

Answer these questions for yourself. Remember, you can be totally honest because only you will see the answers.

- Do your parents use food to punish you?

- Do they make it clear to you why you are being punished and how they would like you to behave in the future?

- How does this make you feel?

- How would you like to feel?

- How could they treat you differently that would be more effective?

- Do you receive food as a reward? From whom? How does this affect the way you think about this person?

- Do you ever feel guilty about accepting or rejecting food? When and why?

- Do you eat only when you are hungry? What emotions do you have at the other times you eat?

- Do you feel trapped or liberated by your eating habits? Or are you indifferent to them?

- Are you happy about the way you eat? If not, can you talk to someone about it?

- Is a family member or friend causing you to turn to food when you are not hungry, or causing you to reject food when you are hungry?

- If so, have you ever told him or her how this makes you feel? Try writing an imaginary letter telling him or her what you would like to say, using one of these sentences:

> It makes me unhappy when...
> I love...
> I am frustrated...
> I am afraid...
> I want...
> I am angry that...
> I feel lonely because...
> I feel...

3 Evaluating Your Weight

What do you see when you look in the mirror? Not quite slim enough? Do you need a few pounds off here, a few inches off there? If only...if only...if only you were slimmer. Then instead of seeing yourself as one of the ugly stepsisters—fat, lazy, and miserable—you would think of yourself as Cinderella, living happily ever after in the arms of a handsome prince.

Just as you inherit your eye color, the shape of your nose, or the texture of your hair from your parents, you also inherit the size and shape of your body.

HEREDITARY FACTORS

Genetics accounts for 60 percent to 90 percent of variations in body size. Genetics determines the enzymes, the balance of hormones, the number of fat cells, and the metabolic rate of your body. Everyone has fat cells. Usually women have more than men, and the fat cells are distributed differently throughout the body. Because they are hereditary, you cannot affect where they go, but you can regulate the amount of fat deposits in your body at any given time by regular exercise.

Having fat cells is normal and healthy and does not mean that you are overweight. Fat cells are necessary for producing sex hormones, regulating metabolism, and providing fuel. They store nutrients in the body and provide insulation. More than a third of our total body fat comes from the foods we eat. An excess of this fat can make us tired and lethargic and clog the blood circulation.

Size and shape are determined by the genes you inherit from your parents, but food and exercise (from jogging to marathon running) play a large role in body size as well. Our eating habits are learned and can be changed. And not only does exercise burn calories, it is also an outlet for emotions.

EACH BODY HAS ITS OWN SET POINT

People who eat a lot get fat, right? Not so. Your weight and shape are controlled mainly by genetics, which determines the body's set point, or desirable body weight. The vast majority of weight loss diets fail because your body fights to return to its set point. The best way to stay at or around your desirable body weight is to eat healthily rather than to eat less.

For six weeks Alicia put herself on a strict diet: no breakfast, soup for lunch, and an apple for dinner. The weight dropped away at first, but then the weight loss seemed to stop. Her body was trying to maintain its set point, which is the genetically determined, natural weight of each individual.

A dieter's weight often rises and falls, sometimes dramatically. This is because the body is trying to return to its set point. Weight is gained when the intake of calories exceeds the output. When you overeat you put on weight, your body temperature rises, and your metabolism increases as the body tries to use its excess calories to return to the set point. The opposite happens when you diet. When your body is undernourished, your metabolism slows down. You feel constantly tired, your body temperature drops, and you sleep more as your body adjusts to fewer calories.

HOW MUCH SHOULD YOU WEIGH?

No chart or table can tell you exactly how much you should weigh. However, experts use a few different methods to estimate a person's approximate ideal weight.

Body Mass Index (BMI)

The body's set point is actually indeterminable because it is completely individual. However, the BMI is one method that is often used to find an approximate set point. The body weight (in kilograms) is divided by the square of the height (in meters).

BMI = Body weight (kg) / Height^2 (m)

The ideal range is 20 to 25. Obesity is said to occur when the BMI is higher than 30.

Desirable Body Weight

Another method often used to find the set point is to start with 100 pounds (for women) and add 5 pounds for every inch over 5 feet. Start with 110 pounds for men and add the same 5 pounds for each additional inch. Remember, though, that this method is extremely rough because it doesn't take into account factors such as the size of your bone structure and the amount of muscle in your body.

Other Considerations

It is worth emphasizing again that the set point is purely individual and is best determined by a healthy diet and regular exercise. Both the BMI and desirable body weight are only rough indicators and do not take the individual body type into account. For example, a larger-boned, healthy, muscular woman might seem to be overweight according to these methods, whereas a smaller-boned woman with little muscle tissue and a lot of fat could have an ordinary BMI.

OVERWEIGHT AND UNHEALTHY ARE NOT THE SAME

More than 50 million Americans are on a diet, 70 percent of families eat low-calorie foods, and health clubs are springing up on every street corner. Still, more Americans are overweight than ever before. What's wrong?

One-third of Americans are said to be obese. A person is considered obese when the body is 20 percent heavier than average (as determined by the desirable body weight method) or when the BMI is greater than 30.

Overweight and obese are very different concepts. The percentage of body fat is a good indicator of this difference. Muscle is four times heavier than fat, so it is likely that a person who exercises regularly and is healthy will weigh much more than a person of similar build who does not exercise and has no muscle tone.

Exercising regularly for thirty minutes a day, combined with an all-around nutritious diet, is the best way to maintain a healthy weight and keep your body at or around its set point. Clinical charts are a rough indicator of your body's set point, but genetics, diet, and exercise are extremely important factors as well.

The best way to determine whether your weight is healthy or unhealthy is to visit a doctor.

STOP HATING YOUR BODY

No matter what your weight and body type, it is important to learn to love your body. After all, it's a part of who you are. When you are feeling inadequate or thinking negatively about your body, try to apologize to yourself for these thoughts, challenge their validity, and then let them go.

Easier said than done? Try a couple of exercises to change the way you see your body. Go to a museum or look through a book of paintings from a different era. Throughout many periods of history, the women who posed for artists would be considered heavy by today's standards. Or rent an old black-and-white movie from the 1930s or '40s.

The most beautiful and seductive actresses of that era were far larger than the tiny waifs we see today. Even so, they are some of the most glamorous, sensuous women of all time.

Throughout history, the image of the beautiful female body has changed radically. Remember this as you evaluate your own appearance and try to appreciate your own unique, individual beauty.

4 What Is an Eating Disorder?

As the media bombard us with images of impossibly thin women and new diet products, the question seems to be not, Why do so many people have eating disorders? but, How can I prevent developing an eating disorder? The National Association of Anorexia Nervosa and Associated Disorders says that seven million women and one million men have an eating disorder. Of these eight million, 86 percent develop their disorder before they are twenty years of age.

Only recently has the relationship between food and family, and even the subject of eating disorders themselves, begun to be taken seriously. The first books on the subject were written in the early eighties. Then, in 1985, singer Karen Carpenter's death from anorexia put eating disorders in the headlines. Women's magazines started to run articles exploring the available statistics and raising the possibility that people who seemed to have everything (money, beauty, success, and power) could actually be missing something important in their lives.

At that time, new research on women was being conducted. Suddenly people were taking a second look at some girls' and women's deep and dangerous desire to be impossibly thin. Physicians and psychologists were discovering that some girls and women had developed extremely unhealthy eating patterns, ones that could cost them their lives. They called these conditions eating disorders.

In this chapter you'll learn about the four most common eating disorders: anorexia nervosa, bulimia nervosa, compulsive eating, and compulsive exercising. As you read, you will notice that there are many similarities between the four disorders. It is important to remember that a person can suffer from more than one eating disorder at the same time.

ANOREXIA NERVOSA

This is the clinical definition of anorexia nervosa, often called simply anorexia:

- ⊙ The refusal to keep body weight at the recommended minimum for one's height and age

- ⊙ The fear of being fat regardless of actual size

- ⊙ The influence of weight and shape on self-opinion

- ⊙ The denial of one's own weight

Food and Your Family

Anorexia is a Greek word, meaning "without appetite" (*orexis*). But anorexia as it is used today is not a lack of appetite. Rather, it is a suppression of appetite. People with anorexia eat very little food or no food at all. They literally starve themselves. They deny hunger pangs but often obsess about food. Some say they spend 75 to 85 percent of the day thinking about food, recipes, or cooking for other people. Food is the first thing they think of in the morning and their last thought before they go to bed. But they don't allow themselves to give in to hunger. Also, most people with anorexia do not have a realistic view of their bodies. They see themselves as fat when the rest of the world sees how thin they are. Thus they continue to starve themselves.

Anorexia usually begins in the teen years or early twenties, when young people are going through dramatic physical and emotional changes. As a teenager you want to fit in, but you also want to stand out. You need to be accepted, but you also want to be liked for being an individual. For a young person, the world is sometimes exciting and full of promise for the future. At other times it's frightening. You may feel the need to create a safe place for yourself—a world of your own that is built to cope with feelings of meaninglessness, low self-esteem, failure, dissatisfaction, and anger. Being a teenager is hard. It is not surprising that 1 to 4 percent of adolescent or young women are anorexic, and the percentage of boys with anorexia is increasing rapidly.

Anorexia is hard work. It takes enormous self-control, discipline, and sacrifice. Achieving this kind of control can make a person feel successful and special and help him or her to cope with feelings of failure or loneliness.

Nya was anorexic. She would get up half an hour before her brothers and sisters on school days just to cook them a big breakfast. She wouldn't eat anything herself, but she would not let her siblings leave for school until they had cleaned their plates.

When Nya finally received treatment for her eating disorder, she told her therapist that she had "food thoughts" running through her mind all day, every day. She was constantly tempted by food because she was so hungry. Part of her would say, "Do, do, do," while the other part would say, "Don't, don't, don't." She was afraid that if she ate even a few bites of food, she would get fat.

The Control Factor

In today's society, weight loss is seen as an admirable achievement. It brings with it attention and recognition. The pursuit of thinness is the pursuit of self-control. By controlling your eating habits, you may feel that you control yourself, your body, your feelings, and the world around you.

As a teenager your changing emotions may be very scary. Many young people do not feel that they have support at home, or that they can talk to anyone about their problems. Some teenagers feel out of control in their lives, and self-imposed discipline seems like a good solution. The rigid discipline that dieting requires restores a sense of control. By denying their cravings for food, hunger pangs, and

Girls and women with anorexia share feelings of imprisonment. They say things such as:

- ⊙ *"I am in prison and can not get out."*

- ⊙ *"I am in my own prison....I have sentenced myself to thinness for life."*

- ⊙ *"I can't see beyond these walls. I don't know how to be normal. I want to be thin, I want to be liked, but I want to eat."*

- ⊙ *"When I eat I feel. It's better if I don't feel. I am too afraid."*

pleasure from eating, teens may feel powerful. It may seem as though ignoring their bodies' demands shows endurance and determination. People with anorexia often feel as though, by controlling their bodies, they are winning power over themselves and the world. However, the eating disorder soon takes control of them, and they feel imprisoned, not free.

"Mind over matter." You have heard parents and teachers say this when you think you can't do something. The brain is very powerful. It sends messages that you should eat. The body needs food for nutrients and energy, and starvation is against your normal instincts. But like those previously mentioned, many young women and men are using their diets to control their emotions. They are afraid that if they allow themselves to eat once, they will lose control forever. They will eat and eat and the pounds will increase. Consequently, as many as 50 percent of anorexics use purging to cope with the stress of eating. They then develop bulimia nervosa.

BULIMIA NERVOSA

The clinical definition of bulimia nervosa, often called simply bulimia, is as follows:

- ⊙ A person eats more in a set period of time than most people would eat in similar circumstances and has a lack of control at the time.

- ⊙ A person has compensatory behavior to prevent weight gain by the use of chemical aids such as laxatives, diuretics, and enemas, or by vomiting or fasting.

- ⊙ This behavior occurs at least twice a week for three months.

- ⊙ The person's view of him or herself is based almost entirely on weight and shape.

Bulimia is more common than anorexia. In fact, because of the rigid discipline required to be anorexic, 50 percent of people with anorexia develop bulimia once the effort of starvation becomes too much. They allow their bodies the food they need and then purge themselves without the fear of gaining weight.

There are two types of bulimics: purging and nonpurging. The purging type compensates for eating binges by vomiting or using laxatives that immediately remove food from the body. The nonpurging type uses excessive exercise or fasting to compensate for the binges.

How Does It All Begin?

Bulimia starts as the regulation of food intake in an effort to lose weight, but it soon becomes a mood regulator. Most binges occur when people are feeling anxious, lonely, sad, angry, or desperate. Bingeing can take one's mind away from his or her problems, but when a person becomes too full, he or she experiences a huge wave of guilt. The fear of being fat returns, and the person purges the food from his or her body.

Maria had few friends. She thought it was because she wasn't pretty enough. She looked at all the popular girls at school and noticed that they were thin. She figured that if she lost weight, she would be popular too.

Maria started to diet. She lost weight quickly, but she didn't win any new friends. One day she went home lonely, miserable, and full of despair. Nobody was home, so she went to the kitchen, opened the refrigerator door, and looked in. She saw a frozen pizza and a half-gallon of ice cream. Maria ate the pizza and then the ice cream.

When she was too full to eat any more, she

was hit by fear. She was afraid of getting fat. So Maria put her fingers down her throat and vomited. She also took some laxative tablets, just to make sure.

Many bulimics describe themselves as "binge eaters" who have tried other ways of dieting without success. The self-image of people with bulimia is similar to anorexics—they both fear fat and feel anxious and inadequate.

Bulimia seems like a solution to some people because they think they can give in to hunger without gaining weight. Some bulimics record eating as much as fifty thousand calories a day, although most binges are between twelve hundred and two thousand calories.

People with bulimia begin a cycle of bingeing and purging in order to lose weight. However, that cycle soon starts to regulate their moods. The bingeing is a way of coping with the world. It makes one feel better and relieves stress, but it also causes guilt. Purging is a way of relieving the guilt. As this cycle increases, it becomes very difficult to stop.

A Shameful Secret

Between 25 and 35 percent of college-age women have used bulimia to control their weight. One major university put up signs asking students to please stop vomiting in the toilets because it was ruining their plumbing. The young women's stomach acid was destroying the pipes.

Bulimia is often easy to keep secret. Its symptoms and effects are not so noticeable as those of anorexia. The urge to binge is uncontrollable, since food is a comfort when bulimics are feeling lonely, sad, or unsure of themselves. It seems to be a solution to confusing emotions. Afterward, people with bulimia often tell themselves, "I won't do it again," because they are ashamed of losing control. But they are unable to stop the cycle of bingeing and purging.

COMPULSIVE EATING

Compulsive eating, often called binge-eating disorder, is characterized by:

⊙ Eating more food in a period of time than is normally consumed under similar circumstances

⊙ Feeling a lack of control while large quantities of food are eaten

⊙ Having a binge that includes at least three of the following: eating rapidly; eating until overfull; eating large amounts when already full; and bingeing in secret followed by guilt, self-disgust, and depression

⊙ Feeling angry with oneself because of the habit of overeating

⊙ Not engaging in any compensatory behavior, such as purging

Leila is nineteen and weighs 180 pounds. She constantly cuts articles out of magazines about different fad diets, and she has tried

them all. She has tried the grapefruit diet, the egg diet—everything.

Yet each time she diets, Leila starts to think of nothing but food after a few days of deprivation. She starts to dream about rich, fattening foods, but she knows she can't eat these foods on her diet. When she steps on the scale and finds that she hasn't lost weight, she feels horrible about herself.

Before she knows it, she finds herself eating whatever she can get her hands on. She eats and eats, satisfying her craving until she is so full that she has to stop. Crying, Leila looks in the mirror and wishes she could be thin. She doesn't know what to do.

It is a common misperception that all compulsive eaters are obese. In fact, only 50 percent of those suffering from this eating disorder are obese. Many compulsive eaters can maintain a normal weight by eating a lowfat diet most of the time and bingeing only occasionally.

What Triggers Compulsive Eating?

Everyone overeats at times, but compulsive eating is different. Compulsive eaters don't eat because they want to; they eat because they cannot stop eating. Compulsive eaters are usually shy, lonely, and lacking self-esteem. They eat to comfort themselves, but the guilt that they feel afterward increases their poor opinion of themselves, setting them up for another binge.

Compulsive eaters eat in secret because they feel

ashamed. They often eat foods that are normally avoided because of high fat or calorie content. In his book *Bulimia Nervosa and Binge Eating*, Peter J. Cooper describes three main triggers for compulsive eating: image, food, and feelings.

Image

Some compulsive eaters start to eat when they think about their weight and shape. They feel fat, hopeless, and depressed, and food gives them the comfort that they need. Some people start to eat when they step on the scale and find that they have actually gained weight, or when they discover that their clothes fit a little more snugly than they remember. When they feel bad about their self-image, food provides instant consolation.

Food

Some compulsive eaters are on diets that are too strict or do not satisfy their hunger. If a compulsive eater diets and is consumed with thoughts of food, breaks a diet, or has fattening foods nearby, he or she is easily tempted to overeat.

Feelings

Some compulsive eaters binge when they don't know how to handle painful emotions. They may feel confused, lonely, or miserable. Maybe they feel as if they have no friends; maybe they are tense before an important test or job interview; or maybe they feel rejected by someone they care about. Food can seem to fill the emptiness inside the person and soothe difficult feelings.

Compulsive eaters also risk developing bulimia.

As they continue to binge, they may feel the need to rid the food from their bodies. They then begin to purge, and the cycle of bulimia begins.

COMPULSIVE EXERCISE

These are the main characteristics of compulsive exercise:

- A high level of activity with little need to rest

- A dependency on exercise to stabilize moods and control self-esteem

- A feeling of being out of control, of being "driven"

- The overuse of the body with the effect of deprivation

It is rare for most people to look in the mirror and think, "Yes, I like what I see." To improve their body, some people prefer to exercise. Moderate and regular exercise is important to keep you healthy. It can also be a good way to lose unwanted pounds. But some people take exercise to dangerous extremes in trying to lose weight. They begin to exercise compulsively—they exercise too often or for extremely long periods of time. Like people who suffer from other eating disorders, compulsive exercisers have a poor self-image and may be dealing with painful emotions. They use excessive exercise to feel as though they are in control of their emotions, their bodies, and their lives.

Dave is a talented quarterback for his high school football team. His family was especially proud of him when he won the "Athlete of the Year" award at school, but they were equally disappointed in him when he didn't win it the next year.

Dave's family was always pushing him to do better and work harder. He never felt as though he was good enough for them, and he decided that he would have to work out more if he wanted to get a scholarship to play football in college. He got up early in the morning and ran four miles before school. After school he went to football practice and then went for another run. He ate dinner in the evening, but he skipped breakfast and lunch to lose weight.

Dave noticed the pounds dropping away. He started to get sick very easily, always catching colds or the flu. He didn't understand why this was happening. He was exercising to get stronger. So why was his body getting weaker?

No Pain, No Gain

Like Dave, who was a successful member of his football team, most compulsive exercisers are normal, healthy, functioning individuals. They are often successful in sports or schoolwork. They usually place a high value on their own achievements and are often perfectionists, independent, and respected by others.

Compulsive exercisers are generally very disciplined. They take this discipline to an extreme, however, until exercise becomes their sole focus in life. Losing weight and getting fit through exercise becomes more important than anything else, including family and friends.

In Dave's case, exercise and diet were combined as a way to lose weight. He cut back on his food in addition to his strict exercise regimen. Compulsive exercisers often suffer from other eating disorders, such as anorexia or bulimia.

TAKING THE NEXT STEP

All of the eating disorders—anorexia, bulimia, compulsive eating, and compulsive exercise—have many things in common. They develop as a way to cope with painful emotions. And regardless of which disorder a person develops, he or she uses food and exercise as a means of gaining control over his or her life. But there's another important common factor. They can all be overcome with help and hard work. It's not easy, but it is possible.

Are you afraid that you may be developing an eating disorder? Do you think you may already have one? Or do you simply want to learn how to manage your weight in a safe and healthy way? Sometimes it is hard to ask for help, especially with sensitive and personal topics like your weight and your self-image. Later in the book, you'll find more about getting help to manage your weight healthily or deal with an eating disorder.

5 Society, Role Models, and Your Body

Why is it that 95 percent of American women say they feel disgust or disappointment with their bodies when they look in the mirror? Why are 70 to 80 percent of fourth-grade girls already on a diet? Why do girls in particular have such difficulty accepting their weight and shape?

Throughout your entire life, you have learned that appearance is important. And, when girls reach adolescence, their appearance becomes more crucial than ever before. Girls learn that there is an acceptable way to look and an ideal kind of beauty to have. That look is dictated by cultural standards and enforced by the media. However, culture's beauty ideal is often impossible to attain. Few people will ever look like the supermodels that grace magazine covers. Usually, the models themselves don't even look that way in real life. But young girls learn that their value depends upon their appearance—an appearance that's often impossible to attain.

IT'S ALL ABOUT ME

Your self-image is how you see yourself in relation to the world. It is affected by everything you come into contact with—your parents, your friends, the media, and the world around you.

One factor that affects your self-image is your body image. Your body image is what you see when you look in the mirror and how you feel about it. What you see can be totally different from your real reflection. Most people have an ideal of how they would like to look. When they see something other than this ideal, they become very critical. Some people see fat where there is none. Others dislike individual body parts, like their nose or thighs. If you don't like what you see in the mirror, it affects both how you feel about yourself and your worth as a person. Your body image affects your self-image.

In turn, your self-image affects your self-esteem. Self-esteem is how you regard yourself and your value as a person. If you have high self-esteem, you'll think you are an important, worthwhile, valuable person. If you have low self-esteem, you'll think you are a bad, lazy, stupid, or worthless person. When your body image does not fit your ideal, your self-esteem suffers. You may doubt your worth as a person, or you may dislike or even hate yourself.

PARENTS ARE POWERFUL ROLE MODELS

Women and girls are much more prone to eating disorders or dissatisfaction with their bodies than boys and men. That's because for females, body image is a very big part of their self-image. And it has a huge effect on their self-esteem. From an early age, girls are taught that how you look is more important than who you are.

The earliest and probably the strongest role models you have are your parents. Parents teach children by example. When it comes to body image, mothers are key role models for girls just as fathers are for boys. Children then imitate their parents; their parents' ways of behaving become their own. Hopefully your parents teach you healthy ways of thinking about yourself, your body, and your weight. Sometimes, however, people learn false, unhealthy, or painful lessons. For example, if a girl sees her mother overeating when she is upset, that girl will have a tendency to do the same. If a boy hears his father call a skinny person "wimpy" or "girly," he will assume that to be a real man one shouldn't be so slim.

Clarissa's mother tells her, "You'll never find a boyfriend if you keep eating those candy bars."

Towanda's father pinches her waist and teases her that she's getting "chubby."

PEER PRESSURE

As you enter your teenage years, you probably notice the power of attractiveness. The popular kids are often the ones who are considered the most attractive. You may know that you fit in somewhere on the scale, but you may not be sure where. Or you may think that you will never measure up, look good enough, or be good enough. Worst of all, your body may not be cooperating with how you would like it to look. In adolescence, the body fat of girls increases, which is a natural part of becoming a woman. However, suddenly gaining weight can be devastating at a time when you are becoming aware of the importance of thinness.

You may be feeling peer pressure to lose weight for the first time. Peer pressure is when people your age try to convince you to do something that you aren't sure you want to do. It can be obvious, such as threatening you in the hallway, or subtle, such as nasty comments or remarks meant to hurt you.

> At lunch one day, Dawn tells Tammy, "You know, with a waistline like that, no way should you be eating those mashed potatoes."
>
> "You need to cut down on those carbohydrates," advises Rae.
>
> "Try working out your abs a little more," adds Hope.
>
> Tammy suddenly doesn't feel hungry anymore.

THE MEDIA MATTERS

Eating disorders are universal, but they are by far the most common in Western society. In the Western world, technology is the most advanced and the most widespread. What people watch on television, read in magazines, and see on the movie screen affects how they live their daily lives. And sometimes it is hard to remember that what the media show you usually isn't real.

On television the news broadcasters are slim

and physically attractive, and the stars of sitcoms and soap operas are beautiful and elegant. In magazines ultrathin models, most of whom are far below normal weight, show you what you should wear and how you should look.

Shop mannequins and Barbie dolls look as though they have the perfect figure for showing off fashionable clothes. No one tells you that if they came alive, they would be so disproportionately thin that they would not be able to walk. Imagine *Beverly Hills 90210* cast with characters that you pass on the street or with whom you go to school. Or think of Sylvester Stallone, who is only five feet, nine inches tall but, due to clever camera angles, seems to have a much larger stature. Everywhere you turn there are images of men and women disguised by makeup; trimmed by personal trainers in the gym; or corrected by plastic surgery, implants, and liposuction. "Thin is in!" the media scream at you. And the pressure is hard to resist.

Family Resource Centre
Hamilton Health Sciences Corporation

HOW DO YOU FEEL ABOUT YOUR BODY?

Take some time and reflect on what you've learned about yourself and your body from parents, friends, and the media:

- When you look in the mirror, how do you feel? Do you like what you see? How would you rate yourself on a scale of one to ten? Why?

- When you are shopping for clothing, are you aware of your body shape? How do you feel about yourself? How do you feel about changing in front of other people? Do you compare yourself to others?

- Do you engage in sports? If not, why not? What would be your real reason for saying no if someone asked you to play tennis or go jogging? If you do play sports, does this improve your body image? What are your feelings about exercise?

- How do you feel around guys (if you are a girl) or girls (if you are a guy)? Are you aware of your body at these times? Do you compete with your friends for attention from the opposite sex?

⊙ Do you think a lot about your appearance? Do you think positively or negatively? What are your main influences for feeling this way?

⊙ How do others see you? What do your parents think about you? How do your friends see you?

⊙ How do you feel about your weight? Do you feel guilty about eating? Are you comfortable with your weight?

⊙ How does your family view weight? How can you express to other people the negative way they make you feel? What changes would you like to make to their views? What would you like to tell them? Write a list of things you would like to say using these sentences:

> I feel...when...
> It hurts me that...
> I want to tell you that...

6 Parents and the Way You Eat

Families learn habits and codes of behavior from one another. How a family expresses love is vital to its well-being. Parents are the role models in families. Most of our parents took their own mother and father as role models, which means that they learned how to love their children by remembering how they were loved. Then they pass on to their children the habits that they have learned from their parents and from their experiences in the world. What your parents learned about weight and food is what they now teach you. If your parents learned unhealthy ways of thinking about their bodies or relating to food, they may pass that behavioral pattern on to you.

WEIGHT-OBSESSED PARENTS

Throughout history women have been starving themselves or altering their natural shape to fit the demands of fashion. The message is that unless you

51

conform to the current standard of beauty, you are imperfect and will never succeed or be loved.

Thus it is not really surprising that our parents are often obsessed with their own weight. They may spend hours either in the gym, poring over calorie charts, checking their reflections, or complaining about their weight. What they don't realize is that they are showing their children that, yes, thin does equal beautiful.

PARENTAL PRESSURE

When your parents are the victims of media messages and pressure from their own peers, they may influence you or even insist that you conform to the same standards. They can place unreasonable demands on you and give you the impression that thinness and appearance are the only measures of success.

> *Julie is sixteen and weighs eighty pounds.*
>
> *She was once a typical teenager who liked to read and draw. In fact, she spent most of her free time at home. She was quiet and shy.*
>
> *A year ago her father, a lawyer for a large company and a regular at the gym, became worried that Julie was spending so much time in her bedroom reading. Although he was glad that she was interested in her books and in learning, he worried that she never exercised. "Hey, bookworm," he would tease her, "you're getting tubby spending all that time in your room."*
>
> *He called Julie "Rubenesque," and "chubby." By making fun of her size, he thought he was encouraging her to exercise and lose weight. He*

was right in thinking that she needed some fresh air and physical activity, but instead of encouraging her, he was being critical and belittling her. Julie's father was not appreciating her for who she was and the things that she did. Instead he was telling her that unless she was thinner, she was just not good enough and would never succeed.

Julie started to believe her father. She began skipping breakfast and lunch and would take laxatives to rid herself of her evening meal. She was influenced by her father to believe the "thin equals beautiful" myth and ended up developing an eating disorder. Now she is severely underweight and has spent time in the hospital for malnutrition.

A MOTHER'S INFLUENCE

A regular customer at a restaurant was pleased to see that her favorite waitress had become pregnant. "Congratulations," she said. "Do you want a boy or a girl?"

"Oh, a boy," replied the waitress. "Life is so hard for girls."

The waitress knows that a mother's role is a tough one. Your mother is often the first one you call when there is a problem and the first person you blame when something goes wrong. It is easy when you are young and dealing with your own changing feelings and emotions to discount her efforts and criticize her for not always fulfilling the role as well as you might wish.

But mothers are doing their best, trying to pass

on the lessons that they themselves have been taught. Sometimes we take them for granted. We do not always show appreciation or recognize their efforts. Then they work harder to be acknowledged and loved for what they do. If they are homemakers, perhaps they will cook an especially elaborate dessert or a new and time-consuming meal. A mother who seeks to be valued through her career may buy gifts for no apparent reason. Regardless, they are going out of their way to win attention.

It is easy to feel unimportant if the people closest to you seem to take you for granted, and mothers often pass on the message to their daughters that they will not be loved for who they are, but rather for how hard they work to seek attention.

Some mothers place high value on their physical beauty and dedicate considerable time to improving their looks. Many were taught by their own mothers that the more conventionally beautiful the woman, the better marriage she will have and, consequently, the happier she will be. Some mothers teach their daughters that the woman who does not care for her appearance will never make a man happy and will ultimately be a failure.

Mothers want the best for their daughters, but the value they often impart is that the normal enjoyment of food—its nutritional importance and pleasant taste—will lead to sloth, fatness, a lack of ambition, shame, and failure.

Amanda, a freshman in college, wrote an entry in her diary about the previous night:
Chocolate. Chocolate. Chocolate. Sweet and forgiving. My best friend. I had a whole box, an

assortment. I bought them two days ago. So expensive.

Everyone had gone to bed. I pulled them out from the bottom drawer. I thought maybe someone had found them. Maybe someone would hear me. But they didn't. I got back in bed, put the box on my knees, and opened the lid. Some of them were wrapped in glistening gold. Some were just there: chocolate, rich and sweet. I took one from the box and let it melt in my mouth. Just one was delicious. A reward.

I took another and heard my mother's voice warning me as I tasted it, "You'll get fat." I heard her again as I slipped the third one into my mouth: "You know what'll happen." And with the fourth she told me, "You'll be fat. You'll be fat and ugly and no one will love you." Her voice rose a notch. "You'll shame your family. People will laugh at you." And with the fifth piece I heard her say, "You're nothing!"

I finished the whole box. Two layers. I did it myself. I was a bad girl. But I don't want to be fat. I want to be loved. I want to be loved the way I love chocolate—ultimately, completely, for who I am!

Then I went downstairs where nobody could hear me and put my fingers down my throat. When I flushed the toilet it was all gone—no guilt, no shame.

SONS VS. DAUGHTERS

Some parents express their preoccupation with weight differently to boys than they do to girls. Boys are often encouraged to eat larger portions of food in order to become "big and strong" or to achieve a "macho" standard. They may fear that if they do not reach this standard, they have failed in the eyes of their parents.

Langston played football throughout high school. His father enrolled him in a county team, and the whole family would turn out to watch him play.

When it came time, Langston applied to the same college that his father had attended. "I'm proud of you, son," his father said, beaming from ear to ear. "Carrying on the Calhoun tradition." He gave Langston a friendly slap on the back. He wanted his son to follow in his footsteps, to win a football scholarship and play for the school's team just as he had years ago.

When Langston did not get a college football scholarship, his father refused to talk to him for a week and instructed his mother not to prepare any meals for him. He said that Langston could take care of himself until he learned that he had "disappointed" his family.

Langston eventually went away to college. At first he played football, but he felt such guilt for failing to get the scholarship that he quit after the first semester.

He turned to food for comfort. When he thought of his family or sports, he would eat a candy bar. During his freshman year, he put on twenty-five pounds and was too ashamed to visit his family that summer. Instead he found an office job near his college and spent

*his days working and his lonely nights eating
and studying.*

*When college started again in the fall,
Langston was even heavier. His friends were concerned and his professors suspicious. The following summer, a caring professor called Langston
into his office and offered to help him find a therapist for his eating disorder.*

*Langston was glad to have a friend and
now visits his therapist regularly. He is starting to cope with his eating disorder and to
learn to value himself despite his father's disappointment.*

As for girls. . .well, they are under pressure to
restrain themselves when it comes to food. Often
baby fat is mistaken for actual fat, and a parent may
impose a diet on her young daughter. This is one
reason that 70 percent of teenage girls have been
on or are currently on a diet.

WHAT A FAMILY SHOULD PROVIDE

No family is perfect, but there are certain qualities
that often characterize a happy, healthy family:

- ⊙ Unconditional love: this is loving each
  other for who we are, not what we
  achieve.

- ⊙ Support: We are encouraged in what
  we want to do or be, but not pushed.
  We are shown differing beauty standards and taught to look inward for

true happiness and beauty. And, of course, we are discouraged from judging our friends or classmates on the basis of physical attributes.

⊙ Listening: Our parents hear and take an interest in what we say and treat our worries, fears, and dreams as valid. If there is a problem that our parents are not equipped to deal with, they listen to the problem and seek out appropriate ways of helping.

⊙ Special attention: Since each child in a family has different abilities, capabilities, fears, and needs, parents respond with various forms or levels of attention. However, too much attention is equally as damaging as too little, because it does not allow for self-development or self-confidence and may eventually cause an eating disorder or make an existing one worse.

LET'S TALK ABOUT IT

When parents are overly concerned with body shape and food, it creates hurt and frustration for their children. You may decide to rebel against their pressure by eating everything you want. Or you may be so influenced by what they teach you that you become a strict dieter from an early age.

It is difficult to believe in your own self-worth as an individual when acceptance from your parents is dependent upon how you look. Parents are role models for their children, and an emphasis on body shape can be a large factor in creating a negative self-image.

Try talking to your parents about this issue. Ask them how important they think physical appearance is. If it is important, why? How do they think this affects you? If it is causing you concern, ask them how they can help you deal with it. Whatever worries you have, it is easier to understand them if you share them with someone else.

USING YOUR DIET TO GET ATTENTION

Food is nurturing. You learn in science class about the vitamins, minerals, protein, carbohydrates, and fats provided by food, but food is also tied intricately to love and sociability.

If you have been abused, victimized, or even the focus of too much attention at home—or if you have been bullied, picked on, or ostracized at school—it is possible that you will deal with the problem by:

⊙ denying your body food. This is self-punishment for not being the popular person that you would like to be.

⊙ searching the cupboards for soft, sweet, sticky foods (particularly ice cream or chocolate) that comfort you and remind you of baby food, and then throwing up to get rid of the guilt.

⊙ bingeing and enjoying the comfortable feeling of food in your stomach, which makes you feel loved.

To deny your body the necessary nutrients is to deny yourself what you need to grow and develop, particularly when you are a teenager and your body is undergoing major emotional and physical changes. Such denial can cause long-term damage. For instance, many girls with anorexia can develop heart and skin probelms. Their menstrual cycles can become disrupted, even stop completely, and require medical attention.

Genie

Genie was the "good child" in her family. She always did what she was told, her grades were very promising, and all the neighbors asked her to baby-sit because she was so reliable. She won prizes at school and was praised by her teachers for her pleasant nature. Her sister, in contrast, won attention for her athletic ability and the rowdy commotions that she caused with her friends.

At fourteen, Genie started to eat less. Her parents and friends noticed that she was losing weight. People began talking about her.

She soon joined her sister in athletic activities, pushing herself to the limits and attracting even more attention. Every morning before school she would go for a run. At lunch, instead of eating with her friends, she would put on her jogging shoes again and take to the streets or play tennis. Instead of trying to be liked for who she was, Genie was engaging in extreme behavior to attract attention.

As a result of lack of food and over-exercising,

Genie's body weight dropped very quickly. After about a year, she stopped getting her period, and normal teenage body development was slowed. Her breasts did not increase in size, and she grew less than an inch that year.

Karl

On the other end of the scale from Genie is Karl, whose parents are so involved in fighting with one another that they do not notice his needs. In fact, they often do not notice him at all. Consequently, Karl turns to donuts and marsh-mallows for love. He binges in secret, turning to a reliable source of comfort.

In addition, Karl is considered the class clown and scapegoat because of his large size. He partly enjoys this because of the attention it brings him and the sympathy he receives from his teachers. But it is a double-edged sword, since the jeers and mockery of his classmates sting very badly. In response to this ostracism, Karl turns again to food for comfort.

WE NEED TO FEEL LOVED FOR WHO WE ARE

We can feel loved for who we are, and we can feel loved for what we do. Maybe your parents are particularly happy when you get good grades in school or achieve notable success with sports. This is normal, and we all need praise for our accomplishments. But you also need to be loved just for being you.

The world can be a difficult place for a teenager

trying to discover her identity. In an attempt to give their children the best opportunities for success, parents may prohibit their teens from expressing their feelings—sexual, emotional, artistic or even political. Although done with the best of intentions, this repression does not boost self-esteem or confidence in a young adult and can often result in a food-as-love substitution:

⊙ It is easy to feel discounted by your friends and family if you are not aware of your own self-worth. Starvation is often used as a way of getting attention and feeling important.

⊙ When parents are repressive—for example, when they prevent a teenager from doing the same things as his friends—over-eating is often a way of rebelling and saying, "Hey, look at me! I need love!"

⊙ An alternative to over-eating, the binge/purge cycle—that is, secretive eating followed by vomiting to relieve the guilt of having eaten foods that you are taught to avoid—is often a silent cry for attention.

TAKING ACTION

Author Nan Fuchs suggests several ways of taking action to dissociate your ideas of food from your need for love.

⊙ Affirmation: Tell yourself that who you are is enough. More importantly, believe it. You do not need to seek attention.

⊙ Getting attention from food: When you accept or reject food, ask yourself if you are doing so because of genuine bodily need or as a way to attract attention—even, perhaps, to cause a disturbance.

⊙ Feeling appreciated: Show others the appreciation that you would like to receive and let the people around you know that you need to be appreciated too.

⊙ Watch motives: If you do not win attention from your ordinary actions, before you turn to or away from food, check how you feel and try to tell yourself that you are good enough as you are. Take control of your feelings by sharing them with others—perhaps a therapist, a teacher, or a trustworthy friend.

EVERYONE IS AFFECTED

In families where one child has an eating disorder, there is a 10 to 20 percent chance that another sibling will also suffer from one and a very high chance that there will be mood or behavior problems among the other children.

If your family is dysfunctional; if the way your family members express emotions is through anger or violence; if there are too few, or too many, boundaries set for behavior; or if your parents put a great emphasis on your school grades or athletic achievements as an indication of your self-worth, then the possibility of someone in your family having an eating disorder is high.

At fifteen, Daphne works hard to win her family's approval. She is the eldest child and has always been praised for her high grades and good behavior. She is the "good girl." She never gets in trouble, and she rarely goes out— and when she does, she is always home by her parents' curfew time.

Her little sister, Caitlyn, the "rebellious one," does not feel the same pressure. She dresses only in black and dyes her hair a different color every week. She goes out with boys and stays out late while Daphne stays home and does her homework.

Although her parents praise Daphne for her hard work, she feels generally unnoticed. Last year she started to cut her intake of food. Nobody really noticed at first, but as the pounds dropped away, her parents started to worry. Teachers began calling home.

Daphne started to get recognition as a result of her actions. She wanted to rebel like Caitlyn and win some attention, even if it was negative.

IT'S ALL IN THE FAMILY

Carolyn Costin, the author of *The Eating Disorder Sourcebook*, cites three reasons why one child in a family might develop an eating disorder.

Scapegoat

When a family is not harmonious, the eating disorder can be used to focus attention away from other problems a family has. Often it brings fighting parents together or distracts them from a sibling's behavioral problems. But gaining attention in a negative way can also create new feelings of hostility and aggression within the family.

Caretaker

In some families, the son or daughter takes on too much responsibility. He or she feels the pressure to be a perfectionist or an overachiever. This is often the case in families where the parents are alcoholics or drug-abusers; one child (usually the eldest) will take charge of the family and put others' needs before his or her own. This is a good quality in itself, but teenagers are developing and discovering themselves, and too much responsibility at a time when they are not mature enough to handle it can lead to an eating disorder. The need for self-control and the struggle for perfection can become self-destructive.

Lost Child

In large families, where there are many problems and a lot of brothers and sisters, the competition for attention can be tough. A lost child copes with family pain and sibling rivalry by simply avoiding the issues. These teens become isolated, shying away from interaction with people because dealing with it is too painful.

By avoiding pain in this way, the lost child risks

a high chance of losing self-esteem. Developing an eating disorder is a common way to use food to deal with emotions, low self-esteem, or inner conflict.

Of course, dieting wins instant approval among our friends and siblings. Daphne, who felt that she was of no consequence in her family, suddenly found herself the center of attention when she became anorexic. She won a lot of attention from her parents and siblings, which gave her a certain amount of power. Unfortunately, she was being rewarded for damaging and unhealthy behavior.

POTENTIAL SOLUTIONS FOR EATING DISORDERS

A problem shared is a problem cut in half, so they say. Sharing through therapy is highly recommended for sufferers of eating disorders. Therapy emphasizes responsibility, relationships, conflict resolution, personal identity, and a change of behavior.

In sessions, Peggy Claude Pierre, founder of the Montreux clinic, works with the understanding that a family is a whole and should be dealt with as such. Other siblings are part of the recovery process too. She says, "The left arm is broken, so we have to pay attention to it. It does not mean that we do not value the right arm or the legs. It's just that the body will work best when every part is healed."

CONTROLLING YOUR DIET/CONTROLLING YOUR LIFE

Seventy percent of teenage girls diet. Seventy-six percent of college males find their body weight less than ideal. During the years between junior high school and college, the pressure to conform to a beauty standard for men and women is at its peak. As a teenager, you may be experiencing pressure to be thin and attractive, to be successful, to do right by your family.

Deana is twenty-one. Her father left her mother many years ago, and her mother brought up a wonderful family of four talented, interesting children by herself. Deana's mother did all she could to make sure her children had the best that she could possibly provide for them. But sometimes she just did too much.

All of her children loved and appreciated Deana's mother and could not wait to tell her about any good news. If one of them was showing talent in a particular subject, Deana's mother would arrange for extra tutoring in that field. If they came home with a low test grade, however, she would immediately schedule a meeting with their principal and teacher.

Deana's sister found she had a talent for painting, so her mother bought her a brand-new easel and a fresh set of paints. Then she signed her up for art class twice a week after school. Deana's sister liked to paint, but just as a hobby. She didn't feel as though she could tell her mother that she didn't like the classes. It would hurt her feelings.

When Deana's brother wanted to start a company but had bad credit, his mother borrowed money from the bank and gave it to him.

He planned to raise the money himself, but his mother wouldn't hear of it. She insisted he take it from her instead.

Deana, a talented musician, had an audition to play for a famous band. Her mother bought her the sheet music and was thrilled to hear her daughter practice. Later, she called the members of the band to tell them about Deana and how hard she was preparing for the audition. Deana was really embarrassed. She felt like a baby and didn't think that the band took her seriously anymore.

Deana's mother was obviously acting with the best intentions, but she did not allow her children to act for themselves. As a teenager, Deana tried to regain control of her life. When she felt inadequate, she would binge. Deana cleared out the refrigerator of all the ice cream, chocolate bars, or rolls of cookie dough that she could find and ate them all. She ate to calm her feeling of inadequacy, then ran to the bathroom to throw up. After purging herself, she felt new again, in control.

As a single parent, Deana's mother devoted all her energies to her children. She had good intentions, but by taking control away from her children, she drove them to seek other means of achieving independence.

Like Deana's mother, most parents have high expectations for their children. Some parents were born into underprivileged families and worked hard to win a respectable standard of living. These parents, in turn, have similar expectations for their own children and can apply extreme pressure on them to succeed socially and financially. Consequently, as their sons or daughters enter the teen years, the typical struggles for independence and autonomy can take the form of an eating disorder, a form of rebellion that also wins the teen special attention.

Strategies for Taking Control of Your Weight

Sometimes it may seem as though your body and your weight are out of your control, but they are not. You can take charge of both your body and your health. To do this, you need some information on what your body needs to stay healthy and functional.

DIET AND NUTRITION

When people hear the word "diet," they often think of restricting food intake in order to lose weight. Actually, that is only one meaning of "diet." Your diet is also what you eat on a regular basis and the way in which you eat it. Your diet affects your weight.

People with eating disorders often have poor diets. Because they do not eat enough healthy foods, they do not meet their bodies' nutritional needs.

If you feel concerned about your eating habits, try healthy food, not diet food, at regular mealtimes. Healthy eating and good nutrition are attainable goals, but they take work. You can also visit your doctor or a nutritionist and have him or her devise a diet plan for you. These professionals can help ensure that you are eating enough food in a healthy and safe way.

WATER, WATER, EVERYWHERE...

Water is the most important part of any diet. You should drink six to eight glasses of water a day, although this may vary according to body weight, shape, and amount of exercise.

VITAMINS AND MINERALS

Vitamins are organic compounds that provide energy and are necessary for chemical reactions that take place in every cell of the body.

Minerals are also important to good health. They are used in the body to make enzymes, hormones, bones, skeletal tissue, teeth, and fluids. The most common minerals are calcium and phosphorus.

Too many vitamins or minerals, as well as too few, can have harmful consequences. If you decide to use vitamin or mineral supplements regularly, it would be wise to consult a nutritionist or doctor. However, a healthy, well-balanced diet should provide the right amount of vitamins and minerals on its own.

CALORIES ARE NOT THE ENEMY

Calories are measures of heat energy. This energy gives you stamina. Your daily intake of calories is

Food and Your Family

completely individual, and you can consult a registered dietitian to determine this level.

Calories come from three different sources: carbohydrates, fats, and proteins. Carbohydrates are converted into sugars in the body. Simple sugars—either processed or those found in fruit—are used up almost immediately during exercise. Alone they are not sufficient for endurance exercise. Complex sugars, on the other hand, are stored as glucose or glycogen, which can be used to support prolonged exercise. Examples of complex sugars are bread, cereals, pasta, fruit, rice, and vegetables.

Fat has a bad reputation as being an enemy of the body. In fact, the body needs fats as insulation and to help process vitamins and minerals. Fat is another fuel used for exercise. Although a lower intake of fat is best, some fats are actually beneficial. The best type are monounsaturated fats, which have the least harmful fatty acids.

Proteins are made up of amino acids, which are used to build muscle. With a higher muscle mass, you burn more fat and carbohydrates, even when you are not exercising.

It is important to balance carbohydrates, fats, and proteins; a registered dietitian can give you a clear idea of which foods contain what nutrients and what proportions are best for your overall bodily balance. Remember that a healthy diet combined with exercise will keep you looking and feeling your best.

The American Heart Association and the Food and Drug Administration recommend a total daily diet that consists of 50 percent carbohydrate, 30 percent fat, and 20 percent protein. When a person exercises regularly, the recommendation changes to 65 percent carbohydrate, 10 percent fat, and 25 percent protein. This is because during exercise your body needs more carbohydrates and proteins for muscle strength and endurance, and the fat is lowered so the blood can pump through your arteries more easily.

CHRONIC DIETING

The belief that one must be thin to be beautiful or accepted often triggers what is known as chronic dieting—where people seem to be on permanent diets. Twenty-five percent of American men and 50 percent of American women are chronic dieters. Dieting is hard work. Dieters tend to have a dichotomous view of food, which means that they divide it into two groups: fattening and non-fattening. This view of food will only create cravings for the "fattening" food that you think should be avoided. When you give in to these cravings, you develop a negative self-image, which puts you on another diet of "nonfattening" foods, and so the cycle begins again.

The answer is to eat right, not less. Start by throwing out your scale—it only sabotages your aim to eat healthily. Also, stop counting calories. Calories are important for your daily energy level, not something to be avoided.

Feeling unhappy with your size? Thinking of dieting? Think first about who gave you these ideas and why. Was it the television? Was it your family or friends? Was it magazines or movie stars?

Was it advertisements? Remember, the diet business is the fastest-growing area of the food industry. Your desire to be thin is worth big bucks to top companies.

TIPS TO TRY

If you think you are dieting too much:

- Try eating six to eight small meals a day rather than three large ones.

- Think of food as medicine. You might not like or want it, but it will help you get better.

- Ignore the voice in your head that is telling you not to eat. Do what you know is right. In this way you will regain control. If you don't eat, food controls you.

- Practice eating at set mealtimes, even if you don't feel like it. This will reestablish regular eating patterns.

- Remember that no food eaten in moderation can make you fat.

If you feel the urge to binge:

- Avoid eating or being around the types of foods that make you feel guilty or can trigger a binge. Eat something else instead.

⊙ After a meal, try involving yourself in an activity or hobby that will distract you from food.

⊙ Resist the voice in your head when it tells you to binge. Tell yourself that you are taking control of your guilt.

⊙ Do not go without food at regular meal-times. If you are hungry, eat until you're full but don't overeat.

EXERCISE

"Go and run around the block," says Mom. "Get yourself off the couch and do something," says Dad.

Exercise, exercise, exercise. We've all heard it: a good run takes your mind off your problems; a game of basketball distracts you; football "knocks it out of you." It is true that exercise is a great emotional release—as long as you don't overexercise. With a reasonable amount, you will not only look good from toning up your muscles, which give you strength and good posture, but you will feel good too. You will increase both your energy level and your ability to concentrate.

At schools, sports and exercise are part of the curriculum. They are meant to provide pleasure and enjoyment. Some school sports are solitary, such as running or tennis, while others are performed in groups and teach the importance of teamwork.

When you are involved in sports, you may be encouraged by your coach to eat a healthy diet and control your body weight. Your coach may also have some good practical advice about healthy living and achieving your peak fitness level.

Exercise Resistance

Rhonda had been on several diets, but none of them seemed to work. She felt fat. She stood on the scale and saw that she was overweight.

She ate six chocolate bars that she had been hiding in her closet, then sat in front of the television with a pint of ice cream. When her father came home, he looked at Rhonda and suggested that maybe she should go out and get a little exercise instead of stuffing her face. Hadn't he even written out an exercise program for her last week?

Rhonda responded by digging deeper into the ice cream tub with her spoon.

Rhonda hated to exercise. She exhibited "exercise resistance," and the pressure from her father to follow the program he had suggested only made her feel resentful and anxious. These are the typical causes of exercise resistance:

⊙ You have a history of failed diets.

⊙ Your parents force you to exercise.

⊙ You have been sexually abused; body size is a defense against unwanted attention.

⊙ You developed large breasts during adolescence. (Large breasts can make athletic activity physically uncomfortable, and teens may also feel emotionally uncomfortable with the dramatic changes their bodies are undergoing.)

FOR HEALTH AND PLEASURE

Women and girls often feel vulnerable and degraded when they are put on an exercise regime as part of a weight loss program. The goal of exercise should be health and pleasure, not image.

"Last summer I cycled two miles to the beach and back twice a week," complained Frankie, "and I never lost an ounce." Exercise doesn't have an instant effect. Muscle has to be built, and stamina has to be developed. Even if you are in a hurry to see and feel big changes in your body, the length and strenuousness of your workouts should be increased very gradually. The idea of "No pain, no gain" is outdated and incorrect, and those video-tapes for "Perfect abs in just two weeks" are scams.

Exercise can be very enjoyable. It is best to find an activity that you have fun doing, and that you will be able to do on a regular basis. There are hundreds of different sports to choose from. Some require money (like tennis or sailing), some are dependent upon geography (like surfing or skiing), and others are accessible to pretty much everyone (like running or basketball). Visit your local library to find lists of groups or clubs, or call your city sports center and see what they have to offer.

It is important to choose a form of exercise that you like—or even choose a few and vary them. The more exercise you get, the more muscles you will work. But don't overdo it. Overexercising is as bad as no exercise; it will drain your body and emotions and eventually make you ill.

LIFESTYLE

Danni was a sophomore in college when she started to confront her anorexia, which had begun when she was fourteen and had become so severe that it was affecting every aspect of her life. She had been denying herself everything because she thought she deserved nothing. She lived alone in an apartment near school. She took a shower once a week and only drove her car for very long trips; otherwise she would walk to save gas and burn calories. Danni set limits for herself on toilet paper and food and refused to watch television. She avoided anything that might be considered luxurious or wasteful.

One day she looked at her life, and an overwhelming sadness came over her. She realized that she had wasted the valuable years of her youth, years that could never be regained.

Danni decided that she was going to be a happier person. She would probably need help, but she recognized that she had a problem and that she would have to be the one to fix it.

Danni called her college counselor and made an appointment. She slunk into the counselor's office, ashamed at her appearance and embarrassed to ask for help. But the counselor understood. She offered Danni the support and care that she needed to change her self-opinion.

Over time Danni learned that she was worthy of friends and that it was okay to drive or shower as much as she wanted. She learned to take control of her emotions and found new ways of dealing with the pain that had been building up since she was a little girl. Gradually the chains of anorexia fell away, and Danni learned a new way of coping that did not involve punishing herself for crimes that she had not committed.

Sukie kept a journal faithfully. She noted her fears and phobias daily. She lived with her younger brother and sister and their father. Her father worked and rarely had time for her, let alone the younger children. When he came home, he only wanted to watch television and eat the dinner he expected to be ready and waiting for him.

Being the eldest child, Sukie felt responsible for the whole family. She cooked and cleaned. After everyone had gone to bed at night, Sukie would check all the doors and windows. She worried constantly about safety; in the middle of the night, she would wake up afraid of fire and check on her brother and sister. She made sure that if anyone had to take a beating, it would be her. She took responsibility for all the mistakes that made her father so angry.

In her journal Sukie wrote that she was suspicious of her neighbors, friends, and teachers. She doubted their motives when they offered help. She was lonely and felt exhausted by the responsibility that she had taken on, yet she always felt as though she wasn't doing enough.

Sukie refused to eat with the family. She punished herself for not being responsible enough by denying herself food. When others had a treat, she would have none. She punished herself for future mistakes as well as what she had done in the past. Sukie denied herself food in the same way that she was denied love.

Eating disorders are "emotional blockers." Thinking about food, counting calories, denying hunger pangs, bingeing, or dreaming of what you would like to eat is much easier than actually dealing with your feelings.

The best way to overcome an eating disorder is not just to eat more or less, but to find a different way to cope with your experiences and emotions. Coping is not easy. You may have years of problems and negative ways of coping built up inside, but you *can* change.

THERAPY

A therapist or support group is a good place to start. Both offer professional advice and understand the complicated issues that you are confronting.

Remember, there is nothing shameful or bad about seeking help. In fact, seeking help shows more maturity and courage than hiding your problems. Finding a therapist or group that you connect with can be the fastest road to recovery.

TRUST

During your teens and early twenties, you will go through enormous changes. Also, the world around you may be changing as well. Your family may split up or experience problems that you do not understand.

In a changing world it may seem hard to trust people, but trust is very important to your recovery. Being able to trust someone means that you have to learn to express yourself. Don't be afraid to make mistakes. Other people may not always understand immediately but once you believe that your feelings are valid, you will find it easier to express them to others.

WRITING

Writing down your feelings before expressing them to others can help you understand yourself more clearly. Keeping a journal can also provide an outlet for your daily fears and problems. By writing down our worries, we can often find a path through what seems like a forest of problems; thus we find new ways to cope and eventually heal.

If you have low self-esteem, it is difficult to remember that your feelings are valid. You could even try writing an imaginary letter to the person who is hurting you, telling them how you feel and why.

TIME FOR YOU

Remember that you are a special person, and take time to do things that make you happy. Do some of these things alone. Keep a list of all of the things you would like to do, and check them off as you do them. Soon you will have a tally of accomplishments: things you have done for yourself that are healthy and remind you of good times.

Say no to people if they ask you to do something that you don't want to do.

Always keep in mind that you, like everyone else, need special attention. Who better to provide it than yourself? Eating disorders or problems with food are rooted in self-esteem, and it can be hard to allow yourself to be treated as someone special, but it is very important to love yourself. Make sure that you do at least one good thing for yourself every day, especially when you think you do not deserve it. Keep a notebook with lists of videos you really want to rent, books you want to read, and places you want to go. Sometimes just getting out of the house to go sit on a bench and listen to your Walkman is enough to remind you of life's finer moments.

COMMUNICATING YOUR NEEDS TO YOUR FAMILY

"I could never explain this to Mom," says Anita, talking about what she sees as her weight problem. "She spends half her time in the supermarket. She just wouldn't understand how I feel."

"I know what you mean," agrees Tina. "My mom laughs at me when I try to talk about weight. She says I've just got a healthy appetite. She's always saying my friends are too thin."

Opening up to your family can be difficult. Your family has been your main influence in life. You are affected by them both genetically and socially. They have taught you how to perceive yourself and the world around you. Even when you leave home, you take those perceptions with you.

Ninety-one percent of bulimics say that their families have either directly or indirectly contributed to their problem. The decision of whether or not to open up to your family members is entirely up to you; you need to assess how they have influenced you and then make your choice. For some people, talking to their family helps. They find loving support. Others, however, meet with rejection and choose to talk to friends, therapists, or social workers instead.

"My mother supports me. She cried when I told her I was bulimic, but she said she would help me. She doesn't put any pressure on me. On Sundays I give her a list of everything I ate that week and why I threw up. I see a look of relief come over her face because she is glad that I can share this with her. I am thankful that she is so understanding."

"When I told my mother that I wanted to lose weight, that I was afraid of being fat and was sick of being laughed at, a hurt look came over her face. She loves to cook for me. I know she wants appreciation, and I think I really insulted her. I'm afraid to bring up the subject again."

"Mom used to have a terrified look on her face at mealtimes. She knew I wouldn't eat

much, but she didn't know what to do. She told me she would do whatever I wanted if it would help. When I finally opened up to her, she was really happy. She said she had thought that bringing up the subject of how thin I was might only make it worse."

"I am afraid to ask for help. My parents think I'm so responsible. I'm scared to let them down."

"Dad really came through for me. I told him that I couldn't cope anymore, and he gave me all the support I needed."

DOUBLE STANDARDS

Your parents set examples, and you learn from their behavior. Sometimes, though, they unconsciously have double standards, meaning that they say one thing but do another. This can be very confusing for children, who look to them for guidance and support. As you get older, that confusion might even develop into anger and resentment toward your parents for not being consistent.

Raj's mom tells him not to eat between meals. She tells him that he should not eat candy because his teeth will rot and that he should not snack because he'll ruin his appetite. But she has few friends herself, and her afternoons seem long with little to do. Raj sees his mom sneak candy bars to comfort herself when she thinks no one is looking.

Raj's mom is not dishonest. She wants him to eat well, but she is sending out conflicting statements. Raj learns that candy is secret and special. He sees his mom coping with her loneliness by eating, and that message overrides her concerns about the effects of candy on his health.

TAKING A LOOK IN THE MIRROR

When Milla told her parents that she was bulimic, they were uncomfortable. Her mother immediately blamed her father, and her father blamed her mother. But the next day they came to her together and thanked her for telling them. They asked her how long she had been bulimic and if she knew why. Her father suggested that they go to a therapy session together because they were a family and they all needed to understand the problem if they were going to cure it.

In order to help their children, parents need to take a look at themselves. They need to examine their own attitudes regarding the issues that concern you, namely self-esteem, weight, and the means of communication within the family.

They probably share many of the same problems as you. When Milla's parents took a look at themselves, her mother realized that her own struggle to attain thinness and beauty had been a negative influence on her daughter. Similarly, her father admitted that by joking about Milla's weight, he was lowering her self-esteem still further.

AUTHORITY

Sonja felt lonely and isolated. She was the only daughter in her family; her two brothers were older and did not seem to take much interest in her.

Her parents always seemed to be yelling. Mom was angry with Dad: He was never home, she took on all the responsibility, he didn't care about them. Why didn't he spend more time with them? What was his problem?

Dad just wanted out. He said he wanted to leave, that he couldn't stand the yelling any-more. Why didn't anyone understand him? He didn't want to come home to this atmosphere every day; what was the point?

There was always yelling. "Go to your room and don't come out until I say so!" shouted Dad when Sonja was caught going out with boys that her parents did not approve of.

Mealtimes were the worst. "Eat everything on your plate," yelled Mom, "or you won't leave the table." Sonja did not understand why finishing her dinner was so important. She pushed her food around and around on her plate but did not eat anything. She was frustrated and lonely. These mealtimes were hell! She decided she wasn't going to eat. Refusing to eat was the only thing she could control amid all the fights and confu-sion. She was not going to be told what to do.

Sonja found that refusing to eat brought her solace. She was hungry, but the hunger pangs were a reminder of her self-control. She was finding a way to cope.

When Sonja's parents finally agreed to go to family therapy, they realized that their means of communication were poor. They admitted that they used arguments and yelling matches to deal with emotional differences instead of listening and trying to understand.

Parents create rules and myths for you to live by. Some of them are obvious, like Sonja's mother telling her to eat everything on her plate if she wants to leave the table. Others are less obvious. Sonja's parents were suggesting to her that problems and emotions can be solved by authority and anger instead of rational discussion, and also that Sonja was not responsible enough to choose which boys she dated.

Sonja's rejection of food became an issue. She was using it as a means of defense, but instead it became an additional problem and served to worsen family relationships.

In family therapy, Sonja's parents learned a great deal about themselves, the rules and myths they created, how they used authority, and the perceptions of image and beauty that they passed on. The family was treated as a whole and the benefits were positive.

Yet this is not always the case. Some families are unapproachable and unwilling to look at themselves or make a change. It is important to assess your family situation and decide if it would be useful to involve them or not. Whatever you do decide, it should not deter you from placing trust in someone you feel would understand.

COMMUNICATION

Whether you have an eating disorder or you are just concerned about your relationship with food, communicating this to someone will ease your problem.

It is not easy to open up. You don't know how someone will react. Some parents will be hurt and feel criticized, while others will be relieved that you want to share your worries with them. Whatever their initial reaction, they will probably need some time to decide how they really feel.

There is no best way to communicate your problems, but preparing yourself with a list of changes you would like to make or information about your concerns will help. For example, pamphlets about eating disorders or suggested recipes for healthier eating might be in order, if you think the family's diet could be improved.

Whatever route you choose, you will probably be taking someone by surprise. Don't expect them to understand immediately. But know that communicating your concerns to someone is a positive step forward.

8

Do You Have an Eating Disorder?

Everybody diets at some point in his or her life, and everyone overeats. Remember your last big holiday meal? Remember how much you ate? Remember the last time you went out with a relative who spoiled you rotten with junk food? This behavior is not an eating disorder. It is normal to overeat sometimes, and it is also normal, though not particularly healthy, to skip an occasional meal.

Sometimes, however, a serious problem does exist.

Every night after supper, Rita would go to the bathroom, turn on the faucet so no one would hear, and throw up. She had read about this way of losing weight about a year ago. The first time she tried it, her throat burned and her nose stung, but she tried again and again. Finally it worked. She could eat the same amount as everyone else and still lose weight. Even better still, she did not have to deal with her mother's worrying about why she was not eating.

Rita obsessed about food. She began to throw up more than once a day. She counted all the calories that she ate and then removed most of them from her body. Whenever she felt depressed or inadequate, she threw up. Rita lost thirty pounds. Her mother was concerned, but her friends admired her. She felt good. And when she did not feel good, she would vomit.

Rita did not realize that she had an eating disorder. She just thought that she was coping. She thought that throwing up was a way of staying thin and releasing tension.

One day her friend Sue gave her a magazine article to read about bulimia and the damage that it does to the body. Rita was stunned. She had developed an eating disorder when originally all she wanted to do was lose weight.

Although it took her more than a year to recognize her eating disorder, Rita knew that she needed to seek help.

WARNING SIGNS

Are you worried about a friend? A brother or sister? Or even yourself? Is someone close to you displaying unusual behavior toward food? Here are some warning signs for recognizing eating disorders. Remember, various disorders sometimes overlap. People with anorexia can purge; people with bulimia can starve themselves. There are no strict rules, only guidelines.

You may be anorexic if you display two or more of the following symptoms:

⊙ You have lost a large amount of weight in a short period of time.

⊙ You deny being hungry and say you are full after eating just a few bites.

⊙ You change your eating habits. For example, you avoid fatty foods, or you eat a greater amount of one type of food (e.g., you eat mainly carrots because you figure they are low in calories).

⊙ You feel afraid of gaining weight.

⊙ You show strange behavior toward food. For example, you often like to cook for other people, but you refuse to eat yourself. You do not like to eat in front of others.

⊙ You have been missing your periods.

⊙ You change your personality or behavior. For example, you become more moody, sensitive, or secretive.

Also, people with anorexia usually wear baggy clothes to hide their overly thin bodies. They may exercise excessively and after a while grow a fine layer of hair all over their bodies.

You may be a compulsive eater if:

⊙ You are constantly concerned with food and dieting, although you do not lose weight.

⊙ You try unsuccessfully to diet.

⊙ You binge and then diet in a cycle.

⊙ You eat in secret (usually large amounts).

⊙ After bingeing you feel ashamed or depressed.

⊙ You eat high-calorie food (that you normally avoid) when you are bingeing.

⊙ You hide the food wrappers from your binge.

You may have bulimia if:

⊙ You have a normal body weight but still think you are fat.

⊙ You try to diet.

⊙ You binge and then diet in a cycle.

⊙ You are secretive about eating.

⊙ You feel depressed or ashamed after bingeing.

⊙ During binges you eat high-calorie food that you normally avoid.

⊙ You conceal the evidence of your binge.

⊙ You try to control your weight by vomiting.

⊙ You binge and then purge yourself by fasting, vomiting, exercise, laxatives, or other means.

⊙ You vomit often.

After a while, bulimics will develop tooth decay as the stomach acid rots their teeth. They will also develop sore throats, mouth ulcers, puffy cheeks, and red eyes. All of these are problems brought on by continued vomiting.

If you think that you may have an eating disorder, tell someone you trust right away. That person can help you find assistance. You should also see a medical doctor and a counselor as soon as possible.

S.O.S.

Rita realized that she was using bulimia not only to lose weight but also as a mood regulator. Whenever she felt depressed or inadequate, she would binge and vomit.

It is estimated that between 15 and 38 percent of college-age females and 2 to 10 percent of college-age males will suffer from some kind of eating disorder. Like Rita, they are trying to cope. Many of them seek help, but for a few the disorder is fatal.

> *Rita's daily vomiting was causing her teeth to rot, even though she always brushed them after she threw up. She had sores in her mouth, the glands in her throat were swollen, and her eyes were often red.*
>
> *Rita did not notice this herself; she was concerned only with her weight and her feelings of inadequacy. When she read about bulimia in the magazine that Sue had given her, she took a look in the mirror and was shocked by what she saw. Her first inclination was to binge for*

*comfort, but instead she told her mother that
she was afraid and needed help.*

SPOTTING THESE SIGNS IN A FRIEND

Do you recognize any of these warning signs in a friend or in a brother or sister? Someone close to you may need your help.

Your approach is very important. No matter what your intentions are, the wrong kind of help can actually cause more damage. It is necessary to remember that the symptoms you see are just the tip of the iceberg. Underneath is a wealth of hurt and pain.

If you are going to approach someone, it is probably a good idea to fully educate yourself first. You can arm yourself with information on where to go for help, but most important, you can provide uncritical support and care.

REMEMBER THIS

The first thing to remember when you are helping someone is that there is very little that you can actually do. You can not force someone with anorexia to eat, you can not stop a bulimic from throwing up, and you can't stop a compulsive eater from eating. The disorder goes much deeper than the symptoms you can see. Eating disorders are emotional problems, and they can not be solved just by eating either more or less.

If the person with the eating disorder is over eighteen he or she can not be forced to seek help. The best you can do is to offer support and encouragement and listen to what they have to say.

When Rita's friend Sue gave her the magazine article to read, Sue said, "I found this interesting. Tell me what you think." Several days later she asked if Rita had read the article and what her opinion was. Sue did not ask Rita any more questions. She did not tell her that she had a problem, but she did show support and kindness. Sue knew that only Rita could cure her disorder.

It is important to remember that only the person with the eating disorder can cure him or herself. Overcoming an eating disorder means changing the way you cope with problems, and only the individual can decide when he or she is ready for this. Any change is going to take a lot of hard work, which will at times be painful.

Armed with knowledge and a positive approach, you should not be afraid to confront someone you care about. He or she may desperately want your help but be afraid to ask for it or even think that he or she does not deserve help.

HOW SERIOUS IS THE PROBLEM?

For advanced cases of anorexia or bulimia, it is important to first stabilize the person's health, as both of these eating disorders can result in severe health problems and, in extreme cases, death.

Stabilization should then be followed by therapy. This is critical since the eating disorder is not just about eating, but about the problems that lie underneath.

For less advanced but no less important cases, it is necessary to get emotional help as soon as possible from a trained therapist, support group, in-patient or outpatient clinic, church group, or any other organization that offers valid support and help.

DOs

If you decide to approach a friend or sibling with an eating disorder, here are a few tips to remember:

- ⊙ Assure them that they are not alone and that you care about them and want to help in any way possible.

- ⊙ Encourage them to seek assistance, providing them with a variety of ways to get that help.

- ⊙ Listen to what they want to tell you rather than giving advice.

- ⊙ Give helpful advice when it is asked for.

When Jody met Chip, she could see that he was a slim guy. He wore baggy clothes like all his buddies, so she did not notice at first just how thin he was.

He was romantic in many ways, but he never took her out for dinner. In fact, she never saw him at mealtimes at all. They would meet for coffee or a soda, but Chip always ordered diet drinks.

Still, things seemed to be going well. Chip was a little aloof, but he was kind. He liked to spend hours hanging out at Jody's house or running on the school track while she was at lacrosse practice. But when mealtimes came around, he would disappear.

On their six-month anniversary, Jody invited Chip over for dinner. She cooked a romantic meal with candles and music. Chip just picked at his food. He ate a few mouthfuls, then pushed his plate aside. "I'm full," he explained. Jody did not understand. She had been shopping and cooking all day. Why didn't he want to eat?

Chip became withdrawn, and Jody started to cry. He left the house and did not call Jody again.

Six weeks later they met in the school cafeteria. Chip had lost even more weight. He looked gaunt and ghostly. Jody summoned up the courage to ask Chip what had happened. "Nothing," he said.

The next day Jody saw Chip racing around and around the track. He looked so thin and fragile, yet he kept on running. Jody started to add things up in her head: Chip never talked about his family; he spent little time at home; she knew he did not get along well with either of his parents; he had a younger brother who was the "golden boy" of the family; she never saw Chip eat; he disguised the size of his body; and he spent hours exercising. Jody began to wonder if Chip had some problems that he had never talked about with her.

Jody went to the library and read a few books on eating disorders. She gathered information and details about places to get help, then went to find Chip. Jody told Chip that she loved him and that she understood if he did not want to continue their relationship, but that she would like him to read the information. Then she handed him all the books and pamphlets that she had collected. Jody told Chip that if he ever wanted to talk or if he needed her support, she would be there for him.

Chip read the books and pamphlets. Several weeks later, there was a knock at her door. Chip was standing there very nervous and anxious, but he told Jody that he would like her help.

Chip is now in therapy. He is learning to eat more and exercise less but it is difficult. He is struggling with his emotional problems, but with the understanding support of Jody, he is winning the battle.

Both Sue and Jody knew that they could not change their friends' behaviors on their own. Rita and Chip had to want to change, but the support of their friends helped them do it.

DON'Ts

Seeing a friend or relative with an eating disorder is difficult. You may wonder what you can do or feel guilty if you think there is nothing you can do. You may be angry, upset, or confused, but do not let your feelings affect the way you talk to the person.

Your friend will probably be offended, angry, or upset when you bring up the subject of his or her eating disorder, but do not react to this person with the same emotions. Do not tell the person what to do or ridicule them. Do not offer ultimatums, such as "I can't be your friend unless…" or "I'm not talking to you until…" Simply let the person know that you will support them in any way possible.

Try to avoid talking about food or weight. This is not the real problem. Certainly do not attempt to force your friend to eat or comment on his or her weight.

Things Not to Say

"Why can't you eat like a normal person?"
If it were that easy, no one would have an eating disorder. Remember that the disorder is a symptom of a much deeper emotional problem. The solution is not simply to eat more or less.

"Stay out of the bathroom!"
"Just eat, will you?"
These are threats, not words of love and support. You can not change someone with threats. There are a lot of mixed emotions involved in eating disorders, and one of the primary ones is guilt. By using threatening words, you will only increase the guilty feelings in the other person, even if it relieves your own frustration.

"Why are you doing this to me?"
"Look what you're doing to your family."
Though friends and family are often deeply affected when someone has an eating disorder, people with these disorders are trying to harm only themselves. This kind of comment just increases their guilt. You are really saying, "Look how miserable you make everyone" and "Don't burden us

with your problems." The person with the eating disorder is suffering very much inside. Take the opportunity to try to understand his or her feelings and what you can do to help.

"What is your problem?"
"Why do you do this to yourself?"
Nobody chooses to have an eating disorder. Such problems are a way of coping with the pain inside—the pain of low self-esteem, guilt, self-hatred, stress, anxiety, and low self-worth. Comments such as these do not help; in fact, they increase the pain. Showing someone respect, care, and love will help in repairing self-esteem and provide support when he or she needs it most.

"Don't you see how unhealthy you look?"
"Being that thin really isn't attractive."
People with eating disorders tend to have distorted ideas about what they look like. Even if you feel you are being honest and helpful, trying to reason with a person who has an eating disorder about what looks ugly or beautiful is not going to accomplish anything. Negative comments about a person's appearance serve no purpose except to hurt them.

"You've put on weight. You look great."
To the person with anorexia or bulimia, this is not a compliment. They do not hear "You look great." They only hear that they have put on weight, which they interpret as "You look fat."

"Go ahead, eat what you want. You're only going to throw it back up, anyway!"

If you have nothing good to say, don't say anything at all. These kinds of comments are cruel and insensitive. People with eating disorders are suffering greatly already. They do not need anyone else to make them feel guilty or ashamed.

"I wish I could be anorexic for a week."
"You must have great willpower. I've tried to starve myself, but I give up after a few hours."
Anorexics do not choose to starve themselves, and living with an eating disorder is not to be wished on anybody. Most anorexics would love to eat "normally" and avoid the emotional and physical pain they feel every day.

People with eating disorders have the best chance for recovery when they are surrounded by love and support. Any kind of improvement to their situation takes a huge amount of hard work over a period of time. Do not underestimate what they are doing to help themselves, and be supportive of their efforts.

RECOGNIZING CODEPENDENCE

If you have decided to help your friend, brother, or sister confront his or her eating disorder and want to be there to support his or her recovery, you will need to be aware of the danger of codependence. This is when you make excuses for, or give in to the excuses of, the person with the eating disorder. By letting him or her slide, you are enabling the person to continue the destructive behavior.

　　Codependence can happen when you try too

hard to help someone else. If someone is trying to help you, you may find that you are misusing their assistance to avoid dealing with your problems.

Bribes, Rewards, and Punishments

"It's so hard to stay focused on getting better," says Tonya. *"Mom wants to help me so much that sometimes it's easier to let her do the worrying. She monitors how much I eat, she bugs me when I don't eat, and she tries to bribe me to do what she wants."*

Tonya's mom is doing her best to help. But she has not learned that her own behavior is very important to her daughter's recovery. "If you eat everything on your plate, I'll take you to a movie later," she says. *Tonya does not eat much. She pushes the food around on her plate and then disappears into the bathroom to throw up the little that she has eaten.*

"That's it!" yells Mom. *"You are grounded for two weeks. No treats if you can't eat like a normal person."*

Bribery, rewards, and punishment do not work. They are not solutions. They focus on food and weight as the issues and actually allow the person with the eating disorder to avoid dealing with the real problem. The real problem is using food as a way of coping with emotional pain.

What Tonya's mother does encourages Tonya not to improve herself. She has low self-esteem to begin with. She thinks she is undeserving of treats, so her mother's punishment actually reinforces her negative self-opinion. At the same time, she is pinning the responsibility of her eating disorder on her mother and continuing to play the role of victim.

Going Out of Your Way to Help

"I won't eat unless you buy my favorite ice cream," says Dylan. So Dylan's mother takes off across town to buy the treat.

It is okay to help someone find foods that they like and do not feel threatened by, but going out of your way to buy them is not a healthy solution. Again, this behavior puts the emphasis on the food, not on the underlying emotional issues.

By asking his mother to go so far out of her way, Dylan is trying to compensate for the lack of love that he feels. He figures that if his mother will go across town just to get him ice cream, she is showing that she loves him. The real solution would be for Dylan to learn to love himself instead of manipulating others to satisfy his insecurity.

Monitoring Someone Else's Behavior

Do not become the "food police." Similarly, do not allow someone else to be your police force. If you have an eating disorder and you want a friend or family member to help you, remember that you are responsible for yourself and your own eating habits. Nobody but you can cure you.

Tonya asked her mom to watch how much she ate and to tell her if she got fat. By doing this, Tonya was depending on her mom to monitor and cope with the problem instead of doing it herself. This also gave Tonya's mom license to punish or reward her daughter for her eating patterns.

Family Eating Patterns

Dylan told his mom that he would not eat unless she drove across town to buy his favorite ice cream. On other occasions he would make breakfast for his brothers. He would cook a large breakfast and insist that they eat everything on their plates, but he would eat nothing. This is a classic example of manipulating the family's eating habits.

No one should change their eating patterns to conform to those of someone with an eating disorder, nor should an eating-disordered person manipulate his or her family's routine. Except in certain cases when a family has an unhealthy diet, it should be assumed that they are the "normal" eaters and that the person with the eating disorder must adapt to and learn their ways of eating.

Setting Limits

"Dad's making me clean the bathroom every day and charging me for food that I binged on was a real help when I was recovering from bulimia," says Martha. Her dad set limits. He did not threaten her or make her feel bad about herself. He did not say that she could not binge or throw up, but he set rules as guidelines for her behavior.

He initially found it hard to set these limits and wondered if he was being cruel when Martha had to pay for food that was missing. Still, he knew that if he allowed her to eat as much as she wanted and not worry about cleaning the bathroom, he was permitting codependent behavior.

Limits should not be imposed as threats or dictated by parents, but agreed upon by everyone as a fair standard.

Ignoring Problems

Ignoring a problem does not make it go away. Ignoring eating disorders allows codependent behavior. Allison was regularly bingeing and purging, leaving her family short of food. Her parents knew what she was doing and hoped that she would stop, but they did not address her behavior. They also ignored the causes of Allison's bulimia: She was having trouble dealing with her family's move to a new state; she had few friends at school; and as her grades got lower she began to doubt her own self-worth.

By ignoring the situation, Allison's parents did not help her to take responsibility for her problem and change it. Allison's eating disorder was not going to go away on its own. She needed help.

Fights

Fighting over food is not a solution. It is just another example of codependent behavior. The real battle should be between you and the eating disorder. Fighting over food is avoiding the real issue while allowing it to continue.

GETTING HELP

If you are concerned that you have an eating disorder, the first step is to tell someone. This is easier said than done. You probably wonder if it is just your imagination. "Maybe no one will believe me," you think. "Will they think I'm crazy?" All of these questions and more will be running through your head. You may be worrying about people's reactions: Will they be angry or frustrated? Will they cry or will they say you are talking nonsense?

When you do decide to tell someone, choose who you would like to talk to. Who do you trust? Who is supportive and understanding? Do you have a close friend who listens well? Many people choose a friend, a relative, a teacher, or the family doctor. If you want to tell your family members but are afraid of their reaction, tell someone else first and bring that person with you when you talk to your family.

You may think twice about telling your family because you are afraid they can't handle it or that they will yell and be angry. But unless you come right out and tell them, you will never know what their reaction will really be. It is a huge risk to take, but it is an important one.

Maybe your family already knows and will be relieved to hear you admit the problem. Or maybe they have no idea and will be very surprised. If this is the case, remember that you are giving them new information that they do not know how to handle. A good idea would be to provide them with books about your particular eating disorder so that they can have a few days to process the information and decide how to deal with it. Giving your family a few days will allow them to get over their initial surprise.

Telling someone about your eating disorder is a very brave move. You will probably feel relieved; an eating disorder creates stress because you are keeping it a secret.

If you do tell someone and after a few days he is still angry or says unkind things, you should remember that it is not his fault. He is not educated on how to behave. Perhaps he just does not want to accept the problem or feels guilty about it. Do not let this prevent you from telling another person who will be more helpful to you.

There is no shame in having an eating disorder; it is your way of coping with your emotions. Still, it is not healthy for your body to continue this behavior, and it is not a solution to your problems.

Some people feel that they are able to cure themselves alone. It may seem hard to ask for help, especially since people with eating disorders tend to be very independent and capable, but it is much easier to become healthy when you share your fears and have other people supporting you of your efforts. Trust is an important part in your recovery. Most important is that you do what you feel is best for you.

Family members are the ideal support system, but if they are not able to help you, you must find someone outside of the family. Seek support until you find someone who will help you overcome your disorder.

WHO, WHAT, AND HOW

Although it may seem as if you are imprisoned by your eating disorder and that the road to recovery is endless, you *can* turn yourself around and regain a healthy life. There are a variety of resources available to help you.

Individual Therapy

In individual therapy you will learn to open up and explore your feelings with the help of a trusted therapist. This may be frightening at first, because you have spent years covering up your emotions and trying to cope with them by bingeing or starving yourself. With the help of a therapist, you will start to understand the origins of your problems, which run much deeper than just food. You will then learn new, more productive ways of coping with your emotions.

Group Therapy

When you have an eating disorder, you probably feel very much alone. You think you are the only person who behaves in this way. By joining a group, you will meet others who think, feel, and behave in a similar way to yourself. Group members usually meet once a week to discuss their patterns of behavior, the ways they are finding to change their behavior, and the issues that create the behavior.

If opening up to one person seems terrifying, then talking about your problems to a group might seem too much, but the benefit of group therapy is that you are surrounded and supported by people who share your problems.

Family Therapy

Often, an eating disorder is an indication of other problems in the family. Alcoholism, substance abuse, sexual abuse, parents arguing or divorcing, difficulty expressing emotions, or negative ways of communicating are just some of the possible underlying causes. For the person with an eating disorder to fully recover, it is necessary for the whole family to look at themselves and their relationships with one another.

Support Groups

These groups are aptly named; they are for support. They are not usually run by a professional person, but by someone who has experienced an eating disorder and wants to provide support and knowledge to others.

Medical Treatment

Confiding in your doctor is a good place to start when you want to tell someone about your eating disorder. A doctor should be knowledgeable about where to go for further help and will be able to monitor your health if your situation is serious.

Nutrition Counseling

A qualified nutritionist will be able to teach you healthy ways of eating that will not leave you afraid of gaining weight or unsure of how to eat right. But remember, eating disorders are your way of coping with emotions, and dietary solutions will only deal with part of the problem.

THE LAST WORD ON HELP

Whomever you decide to tell, whatever route you choose for recovery, however serious you think your problem is, it is important that you tell someone you can trust and ask them to help and support you in your efforts to get healthy again. Do not think that your problem is not important or serious enough. If you are having trouble coping with your emotions or you feel that your situation at home is causing you difficulties, it is vital that you talk to someone. However small your problem may seem, you must learn to deal with it now before it gets worse.

9 Tips for Healthy Eating

Why do some people resist eating all day, with constant "food thoughts" on their minds—only to binge on chips, candy, pasta, and anything else that they can get their hands on? Why does certain people's weight drop a few pounds and then plateau? Why is it that 95 percent of dieters gain back the weight that they have fought so hard to lose?

Because diets do not work.

There is not simply one "correct" way to eat. There is a recommended balance of carbohydrates, proteins, and fats, and there is a suggested standard of three meals per day. But there are no hard-and-fast rules, which means that how and what you eat are personal choices that involve making responsible decisions.

Making decisions about food can be difficult, especially when you feel silent pressure from your friends, family, or the media to conform to an ideal based on appearance rather than health.

Remember, the easiest way to look and feel great is to eat healthily and exercise regularly.

MAKING A PLAN

Making a plan means changing the way you view food. Food is neither the enemy nor a friend. Its most important quality is that it provides the necessary fuel for your body to function properly. Denying this fact may mean that your body will eventually suffer stress and long-term damage.

When making a plan, list the foods that seem to provoke a binge or create a fear of gaining weight. Avoid these foods at first. It does not matter if they are good or bad for you; they can be reintroduced into your eating pattern at a later date. The idea is to concentrate on eating food in a balanced way to build a healthy body.

Your plan should include three meals per day, with an optional two to three healthy snacks (for example, fruit or balanced sports bars). The American Heart Association and the FDA suggest that your meals be a balance of 50 percent carbohydrate, 30 percent fat, and 20 percent protein.

FOOD BASICS

Good eating should happen without guilt or binges. It means maintaining a healthy diet. National surveys show that the average teen diet is high in total fat, saturated fat, cholesterol, sodium, and sugar; it is low in dietary fiber, folate, vitamin A, vitamin E, vitamin B_6, iron, calcium, zinc, and magnesium. If you think that the four basic food groups are fast, fried, fatty, and frozen, or that the best meal is no meal at all, then it is time to make some changes. The first step toward a healthy, balanced diet is learning some food basics.

Carbohydrates are your simplest energy source. They are found in whole-grain breads, pasta, rice, and potatoes. Carbohydrates do not necessarily make you gain weight. They become a problem only when people consume excessive amounts of them. When too many carbohydrates are eaten to be used up right away, the body stores those calories as fat. The right amount of carbohydrates are a source of energy necessary to get you through the day. Insufficient carbohydrates will leave you tired and run-down.

Protein is also a potential source of energy, but when you eat sufficient carbohydrates, proteins will be used for building and repairing body tissue and maintaining the body's immune system.

Fat is a necessary part of your daily diet. There are many different kinds of fats that have various effects on your body. Some of these effects are beneficial. Fats from avocados, olive oil, fish, or nuts are important for absorbing fat-soluble vitamins and fatty acids. HDL (high-density lipoprotein) is a form of cholesterol found in fish like salmon and tuna that actually helps to clean out your arteries. It also slows down the emptying of the stomach so you feel full longer.

Of course, there are also bad fats. Saturated fats and LDL (low-density lipoprotein), found in junk foods like candy bars, french fries, and fatty red meat, can clog arteries and increase your blood cholesterol level. All fats have a lot of calories and can cause weight gain if eaten in excess, but saturated fats are especially hard for your body to break down and use as energy.

If you eat healthy, balanced meals made with fresh foods, you should not have to worry too much about fats.

Vitamins, **minerals**, and **fiber** are important components of the foods you eat. Vitamins and minerals are essential to the body's regulation of the immune and nervous systems. We are still learning about the specific functions of the various vitamins and minerals, but we do know certain things already. For example, vitamin C boosts your immune system; iron is essential to the blood's ability to carry oxygen; calcium is needed for strong bones; and vitamin E helps maintain healthy hair and skin. The list goes on and on. The most important thing to remember is, of course, that a balanced diet made up of fresh fruits and vegetables, low-fat meats, and dairy products will provide the necessary nutrients.

Fiber is an essential part of the diet because it helps to clean out the digestive tract and lowers blood cholesterol. It also helps to make you feel full. Fiber can be found in fruits, vegetables, and whole grains.

SATISFYING THE HUNGER

You probably know most of these basic facts about food already. Most people are aware of what constitutes a healthy diet, but few use it as a standard. Why? Because in our society, food represents more than fuel—it represents love.

A thin body is held up as the only desirable way to be. This makes weight loss seem like a form of self-improvement, an answer to your problems, a substitute for the self-confidence and love that are missing in your life. We are often trained to think that only thin people deserve love.

Food also represents love because it is present in so many expressions of affection. People often show love by giving food. Whether it's a big family meal at Grandma's house or a box of chocolates from a sweetheart, we learn to feel loved when we eat. As a result we often eat to feel loved.

There are two types of hunger: physical hunger, which you feel when your body needs food for fuel; and emotional hunger, which results from cravings for things that are missing from your life, such as love, understanding, happiness, and security.

Some people treat these two types of hunger as the same thing and use food to satisfy both simultaneously. Being able to separate the two hungers is one step toward overcoming an eating disorder.

GETTING PAST FOOD FEARS

To get past your food fears, try some of these tips:

- ⊙ Eat for health, not diet.

- ⊙ Experiment with different flavors and styles of foods. Risk helps develop feelings of competence and achievement.

- ⊙ Trust yourself to eat until you are full and then to stop.

⊙ Tell yourself that you deserve the best and eat the things that you enjoy.

⊙ Allow yourself to eat other people's cooking.

⊙ Talk about your thoughts, fears, and worries with someone you trust.

There are many myths and rules about eating and food—myths and rules set by society that suggest that thinness and abstinence from food are attractive qualities that will make you more desirable, successful, in control, and therefore happy. Food is seen as either good or bad on the basis of whether it causes weight gain or loss. Manipulating your food can, with great effort, change your body size to some degree, but it cannot change who you are. Learning to appreciate, and like, the real you will have a lasting impact on yourself and others around you. The goal is to be able to look at food objectively, not emotionally. To be a healthy eater, you must learn to eat without fear.

Glossary

anorexia nervosa An eating disorder that drives people to lose large amounts of weight as a means of dealing with emotional problems.

body-image The way you feel about your body, how fat or thin you think you are, and how important this is to you.

body mass index Your body weight (in kilograms) divided by the square of your height (in meters). The result of this sum should be between 20 and 25 for the average healthy person.

bulimia An eating disorder that drives a person to binge and purge in cycles as a way to deal with emotions.

codependence A situation in which two people rely on each other's needs to validate themselves.

comfort foods Soft, sweet, usually fatty foods eaten to fill an emotional void.

compulsive eating An eating disorder in which a person eats large amounts of food, usually comfort food, to fill an emotional void.

Food and Your Family

compulsive exercising A disorder in which a person exercises beyond the body's healthy limits.

diuretics Medications used to dispel water from the body.

dysfunctional families Families that have difficulty expressing emotions in a healthy way, or have other problems such as alcoholism, drug addiction, or sexual abuse.

emetics Medications that induce vomiting.

laxatives Medications used to ease constipation and help rid the body of food through the bowels.

purge To rid the body of food before it has been digested.

role models Important people in your life who influence the way you think.

self-esteem How you feel about yourself in the world.

set point Your body's natural weight.

Where to Go for Help

The American Anorexia/Bulimia Association, Inc.
(AABA)
165 West 46th Street, Suite 1108
New York, NY 10036
(212) 575-6200
Web site: http://members.aol.com/amanbu

American Dietetic Association
216 West Jackson Boulevard, Suite 805
Chicago, IL 60606
(312) 899-0040
Nutrition Hotline: (800) 366-1655
Web site: http://www.eatright.org

Anorexia Nervosa and Related Eating Disorders,
Inc. (ANRED)
P.O. Box 5102
Eugene, OR 97405
(541) 344-1144
Web site: http://www.anred.com

119

Center for the Study of Anorexia and Bulimia (CSAB)
c/o The Institute for Contemporary Psychotherapy
1841 Broadway, Fourth Floor
New York, NY 10023
(212) 333-3444
Web site: http://www.icpnyc.org/treatment/csab.html

Eating Disorders Awareness and Prevention, Inc.
(EDAP)
603 Stewart Street, Suite 603
Seattle, WA 98101
(206) 382-3587
Web site: http://members.aol.com/edapinc

Helping to End Eating Disorders
9620 Church Avenue
Brooklyn, NY 11212
(718) 240-6451
(718) 934-3853
Web site: http://www.eatingdis.com

National Association of Anorexia Nervosa and Associated Disorders (ANAD)
P.O. Box 7
Highland Park, IL 60035
Hotline: (847) 831-3438
Web site: http://members.aol.com/anad20/index.html

National Eating Disorders Organization (NEDO)
6655 South Yale Avenue
Tulsa, OK 74136
(918) 481-4044
Web site: http://www.laureate.com

Overeaters Anonymous (OA)
P.O. Box 44020
Rio Rancho, NM 87174
(505) 891-2664
Web site: http://www.overeatersanonymous.org

Weight Control Information Network
1 WIN Way
Bethesda, MD 20892-3665
(301) 984-7378
(800) WIN-8098
Web site:
http://www.niddk.nih.gov/health/nutrit/win.htm

IN CANADA

Anorexia Nervosa and Associated Disorders (ANAD)
109-2040 West Twelfth Avenue
Vancouver, BC V6J 2G2
(604) 739-2070

The National Eating Disorder Information Centre
College Wing, First Floor, Room 211
200 Elizabeth Street
Toronto, ON M5G 2C4
(416) 340-4156
Web site: http://www.nedic.on.ca

WEB SITES

http://www.mirror-mirror.org
http://www.somethingfishy.com
http://www.fda.gov/opacom/catalog/eatdis.html

For Further Reading

Berg, Frances. *Afraid to Eat: Children and Teens in Weight Crisis.* Hettinger, ND: Healthy Weight Publishing Network, 1997.

Berry, Joy. *Good Answers to Tough Questions About Weight Problems and Eating Disorders.* Chicago: Children's Press, 1991.

Boskind-White, Marlen, et al. *Bulimarexia: The Binge/Purge Cycle.* New York: W. W. Norton & Co., 1991.

Bruch, Hilde. *Eating Disorders: Obesity, Anorexia Nervosa, and the Person Within.* New York: Basic Books, 1985.

Burby, Liz. *Bulimia Nervosa: The Secret Cycle of Bingeing and Purging.* New York: The Rosen Publishing Group, 1998.

Costin, Carolyn. *The Eating Disorder Sourcebook.* Los Angeles: Lowell House, 1997.

Crook, Marion. *Looking Good: Teenagers and Eating Disorders.* Toronto: NC Press, Ltd., 1992.

Hall, Lindsey, et al. *Bulimia: A Guide to Recovery: Understanding & Overcoming the Binge-Purge Syndrome.* Carlsbad, CA: Gurze Books, 1992.

Hall, Liza F. *Perk! The Story of a Teenager with Bulimia.* Carlsbad, CA: Gurze Books, 1997.

Hornbacher, Marya. *Wasted: A Memoir of Anorexia and Bulimia.* New York: HarperCollins, 1998.

Jantz, Gregory L. *Hope, Help, and Healing for Eating Disorders.* Wheaton, IL: Harold Shaw Publishers, 1995.

Kolodny, Nancy J. *When Food's a Foe: How You Can Confront and Conquer Your Eating Disorder.* New York: Little, Brown, and Company, 1992.

Maine, Margo, and Craig Johnson. *Father Hunger: Fathers, Daughters, and Food.* Carlsbad, CA: Gurze Books, 1991.

Maloney, Michael, and Rachel Kranz. *Straight Talk About Eating Disorders.* New York: Facts on File, 1991.

Meltsner, Susan. *Body and Soul: A Guide to Lasting Recovery from Compulsive Eating and Bulimia.* New York: Fine Communications, 1997.

Newman, Leslea. *Eating Our Hearts Out: Personal Accounts of Women's Relationship to Food.* Freedom, CA: Crossing Press, 1993.

Rankenberger, Elizabeth. *Food and Love: Dealing with Family Attitudes About Weight.* New York: The Rosen Publishing Group, 1998.

Smith, Chelsea, and Beverly Runyon. *Diary of an Eating Disorder: A Mother and Daughter Share Their Healing Journey.* Dallas, TX: Taylor, 1998.

Smith, Erica. *Anorexia Nervosa: When Food Is The Enemy.* New York: The Rosen Publishing Group, 1999.

Ward, Christie. *Compulsive Eating: The Struggle to Feed the Hunger Inside.* New York: The Rosen Publishing Group, 1998.

Zimmer, Marc, and Ira M. Sacker. *Dying to Be Thin: Understanding & Defeating Anorexia & Bulimia.* New York: Warner Books, 1995.

Index